DIVINE EDUCATORS

Farnaz Maʿṣúmián has a Master's degree in Middle Eastern Studies from the University of Texas at Austin with emphasis in world religions. Her Master's research was published as *Life After Death: A Study of the Afterlife in World Religions* (OneWorld, 1995; Kalimát, 2002) and won first prize in the religion/spirituality category at the Beijing International Book Fair in 1998. It has since been translated into several other languages. Farnaz has taught World Religions for 13 years and now teaches at the University of Texas at Austin. Her primary research interest is in the eschatology of world religions.

Bijan Maʿṣúmián has a Ph.D. in Curriculum Development with emphasis in Instructional Technology from the University of Texas at Austin. His professional focus is in diverse applications of computer technology in human learning. He is the Manager of Global Learning Technologies at AMD (Advanced Micro Devices), a leading global manufacturer of microprocessors. Bijan has been studying world religions for the past 15 years. His current research is focused on interfaith dialogue and its potential contributions to religious reconciliation and the promotion of world peace.

DIVINE EDUCATORS

by

Farnaz and Bijan Ma‘ṣúmián

GEORGE RONALD • OXFORD

George Ronald, Publisher
Oxford
www.grbooks.com

ISBN 0-85398-499-9

A catalogue record for this book is available from the British Library

To our parents
and to the indomitable spirits of
Golnár Sahbá
and
Muhammad Shaykhzádeh

Contents

These Mirrors will everlastingly
succeed each other, and will continue
to reflect the light of the Ancient of
Days . . . for the Grace of God can
never cease from flowing.

Bahá'u'lláh

Preface

In a world where terrorism has led to misunderstandings about the true nature of religion, many people are either becoming entrenched in religious fundamentalism of one kind or another, or are turning away from religion altogether. Both are a tragedy, leaving millions worldwide without access to the spiritual heritage of humanity.

Religious tolerance has emerged as a major issue in the early 21st century. It is on the agenda of governments as never before. Religious extremism takes many forms worldwide; centuries-old distrust, simmering under the surface of civilized society, has a way of suddenly exploding into hatred and violence. Although this has happened more times than the world cares to remember, perhaps the incident that most dramatically brought the world up short was the attack on 11 September 2001 in the United States.

Subsequent attacks around the world have kept the problem of religious extremism in the news. "September 11th" has long been overshadowed by the suffering of countless victims worldwide. But still, it will perhaps be forever etched in the collective memory of humanity as a day when the new wave of religious extremism took the lives of thousands of innocent victims. Yet that terrible day of wrath and hatred was also the 108th anniversary of another significant event on American soil characterized, ironically, by a quest for harmony and religious reconciliation.

On 11 September 1893, about 1,500 miles from the future site of the Twin Towers, the first Parliament of Religions was inaugurated in Chicago as part of the World's Columbian

Exposition. On that memorable day, the Columbian Liberty Bell sounded ten times in honor of the presence of representatives from ten of the great religions of the time. The world had never witnessed a scene quite like this. The multitude of visitors and participants at the Parliament were awe-struck by what they witnessed on that day – perhaps the very first organized parade of religious diversity in human history.

> The ocher robes of Buddhist ascetics, the vermilion cloaks and turbans of Hindu swamis, the silk vestments of Confucians, Taoists, and Shinto priests, the somber garb of Protestant ministers, all gathered together on the platform around a Roman Catholic cardinal, dressed in scarlet and seated in a high chair of state . . . Over and over again, the throng burst into tumultuous applause. The waving handkerchiefs, and mingling tears and smiles combined to make a scene never to be forgotten.[1]

The next day, the *Chicago Tribune* captured the enthusiastic mood of the crowd by declaring that people from "the four corners of the world had come together to forward the cause of a common humanity here and hereafter."[2]

Sadly, the loving spirit that led to the holding of that watershed event, and all the subsequent noble attempts at interfaith dialogue and religious reconciliation since, including a second Parliament of Religions on the 100th anniversary of the first one, failed to prevent the 9/11 disaster, as they have failed to prevent countless acts of war, murder and genocide fueled by religious hatred. Yet today, and regardless of religious affiliation, most people still appear committed to the noble ideals of the presenters and participants at the two Parliaments and seem determined to thwart attempts by a small minority of extremists in different religions to hold their rich traditions hostage to questionable plans and motives.

Continued religious strife in different parts of the world,

the rise of militancy and global terrorism all suggest a bleak and gloomy future for humanity. Yet other indicators point to a brighter future with the dawn of an "ecumenical age" and growing acceptance of religious pluralism as a sign of social civility worldwide.

Numerous factors have contributed to this positive development. Foremost among these are the giant leaps in science and technology that have enabled people of diverse cultures and faiths to come into contact with each other and engage in massive exchanges of various kinds all over the globe. Our planet has practically shrunk into a global village whose inhabitants are now becoming increasingly aware of the wide range of belief systems held throughout the world. The phenomenal growth of the internet, that has thrown a blanket of knowledge and information over the entire planet, is also providing unprecedented impetus for collaborative efforts among people of diverse backgrounds.

In the religious domain, socially active groups are now regularly co-sponsoring humanitarian projects aimed at improving the quality of life at local, regional, national, and global levels. These include attempts to "make poverty history" by providing opportunities for education and decent work, building homes for the homeless, resettling refugees, supporting victims of violence, mentoring delinquent juveniles, fostering initiatives for racial reconciliation, and so on. These and similar worthy projects are leading to more frequent collaboration and dialogue among people of diverse backgrounds and helping to promote goodwill and improved understanding of different cultures and religions.

The constructive efforts of religious groups have been reinforced by contributions from several renowned scholars of comparative religion whose research has provided a theoretical framework for a more pluralist and collaborative view of religion. Among these, John Hick, Raimundo Panikkar, Wilfred Cantwell Smith, Paul Knitter, Hans Küng and Diana

Eck have called for an end to proclamations of religious exclusivity and claims of superiority of one belief system over others. While recognizing the existing divergences in religious systems of the world, these authors argue that all the great religions also provide insights and wisdom that should be taken advantage of to help improve the human condition. Smith is even promoting the idea of a "world theology" that recognizes the unique contributions of each major religion and yet is broad enough to value and embrace the entire religious experience of humankind.[3] The governing body of the Bahá'í Faith has in a recent statement characterized the founders of the world religions as the "spiritual Educators of history, as the animating forces in the rise of the civilizations through which consciousness has flowered . . . In loving them humanity has progressively learned what it means to love God."[4]

Other scholars who share these views are convinced that a new age of religious pluralism and interfaith dialogue is now upon us. They believe that, as participants in these exchanges penetrate beneath superficial doctrinal disagreements, they will discover vast grounds of accord among their respective traditions. Andrew Wilson's massive collection of sacred literature from around the world showing common themes and patterns in world religions seems to provide scriptural support for this position.[5]

In writing this book, therefore, we have been not only spurred on by the current crisis in religious prejudice, but also encouraged by the increasing realization both by scholars and by the masses of ordinary people that despite diverse, sometimes conflicting, cultural expressions and human interpretations, all the great religious traditions of the world share a common foundation that fosters love, unity, and brotherhood.

Any substantive interfaith dialogue for identifying common ground among religions must start with an examination of the history and primary scriptures of different traditions, as these provide the foundation for beliefs and practices of the faithful.

Even a cursory look at the history and sacred literature of the major world religions reveals similarities in at least three areas.

First, there is clear emphasis on the sanctification of human character. All religious traditions encourage their followers to acquire or manifest timeless virtues such as love, selflessness, honesty, justice, truthfulness, compassion, righteousness, and so on.

Second, a study of the lives of the founders of most religions – insofar as this is possible – suggests that these individuals have undergone remarkably similar experiences. For instance, they all took upon themselves the task of providing spiritual guidance to their contemporaries. All suffered persecution and rejection by the people of their time. In many cases, such opposition was instigated or assisted by the divines or leaders of their mother religion. Most went through a purification during which they had to struggle with the promptings of the "devil" and obtained victory over evil or satanic powers. In the face of adversity, they all demonstrated exemplary courage and sacrificed their comfort for the edification and enlightenment of their fellow human beings. While they all spoke with spiritual authority, they also demonstrated love, wisdom, peacefulness, gentleness, and compassion for all.

Third, a close scrutiny of the deeds and words of these spiritual educators seems to point to the existence of a dual nature in them: human and divine. In their human nature, they appear to be mere mortals like the rest of us. Their bodies experience the same feelings and needs as others. In their divine nature, however, they are presented as elevated above the world of humanity, invested with a unique capacity to receive divine revelation and convey transformative guidance to the masses. To draw on a metaphor explained more fully on pages 30, 35–6 and 94, they may be understood as perfect mirrors reflecting the same divine image to all those who care to look. Each of them also comes from a mother religion whose tradition is closely woven into the fabric of the new religion He establishes.

The primary goal of this book is to expand on the above themes in an attempt to provide scriptural and historical evidence for commonalities in the lives, characters, and teachings of the central figures of seven world religions: Hinduism, Buddhism, Zoroastrianism, Judaism, Christianity, Islam and the Bahá'í Faith. Each chapter begins with a brief introduction of the subject, and then presents passages from the sources of each religious tradition. Most of these are primary texts such as the Bhagavad Gita, the Dhammapadha, the Gathas, the Hebrew Bible, the Gospels, the Qur'án, or the Writings of Bahá'u'lláh. At times secondary sources such as Islamic traditions (*hadith*) have been used.

We hope that this introductory volume will generate additional interest in the subject and further the cause of interfaith dialogue and understanding throughout the world.

Advents: Their Appearance Prophesied

The scriptures of most religions tell of holy figures who recognize the station and destiny of the divine educators years before the start of their ministries.

Buddhism

Various stories and legends are connected with the birth of Buddha. His mother is believed to have dreamed that the future Buddha has entered her womb in the form of a sacred elephant *(see page 123)**. Another account notes that, after His birth in the Lumbini garden, His father calls in a wise and learned Brahmin (a Hindu priest,* rishi*) who is skilled in interpreting signs, and asks him to examine the newborn child and tell of His future.*

> Now there was at that time in a grove near Lumbini, Asita, a rishi, leading the life of a hermit. He was a Brahman of dignified mien, famed not only for wisdom and scholarship, but also for his skill in the interpretation of signs. And the king invited him to see the royal babe . . .
>
> The seer, beholding the prince, wept and sighed deeply. And when the king saw the tears of Asita he became alarmed and asked: "Why has the sight of my son caused thee grief and pain?"
>
> But Asita's heart rejoiced, and, knowing the king's mind to be perplexed, he addressed him, saying:
>
> ". . . Banish all anxiety and doubt . . . the child now born will bring deliverance to the whole world.

"Recollecting that I myself am old, on that account I could not hold my tears; for now my end is coming on and I shall not see the glory of this babe. For this son of thine will rule the world . . .

"He will either be a king of kings to govern all the lands of the earth, or verily will become a Buddha . . .

"On the fire of covetousness he will cause the cloud of his mercy to rise, so that the rain of the law may extinguish it. The heavy gates of despondency will he open, and give deliverance to all creatures ensnared in the self-entwined meshes of folly and ignorance."

. . . When the royal parents heard Asita's words they rejoiced in their hearts and named their new-born infant Siddhatta, that is, "he who has accomplished his purpose . . ."[1]

Christianity

The Gospels maintain that there is a passage in the book of Isaiah that specifically refers to the appearance of Jesus. In this passage, the Lord promises the appearance of a child from a virgin or young woman as a sign to Ahaz, the King of Judah.

Therefore the Lord himself shall give you a sign; Behold a virgin shall conceive, and bear a son, and shall call his name Emmanuel (God with us).[2]

Matthew relates that a caring Joseph is contemplating a quiet separation from the recently pregnant Mary to avoid putting her to shame, when an angel of the Lord appears to him in a dream and gives him the glad-tidings that the baby has been conceived through the intervention of the Holy Spirit.

Now the birth of Jesus Christ was on this wise: When as his mother Mary was espoused to Joseph, before they came together, she was found with child of the Holy Ghost. Then Joseph her husband, being a just man, and not willing to make her a public example, was minded to put her away privily. But while he thought on these things, behold, the angel of the Lord appeared unto him in a dream, saying, Joseph, thou son of David, fear not to take unto thee Mary thy wife: for that which is conceived in her is of the Holy Ghost. And she shall bring forth a son, and thou shalt call His name JESUS: for he shall save his people from their sins.

Now all this was done, that it might be fulfilled which was spoken of the Lord by the prophet, saying, Behold, a virgin shall be with child, and shall bring forth a son, and they shall call His name Emmanuel, which being interpreted is, God with us.[3]

Matthew (2: 1-12) tells of three wise men (Magi) from the East who follow a star and travel to Bethlehem to pay homage to the newborn Jesus, bringing Him gifts of gold, frankincense and myrrh. The Magi were, more than likely, Zoroastrians. To this day, frankincense and myrrh are offered at the altars of Zoroastrian temples. The roots of the story of the Magi can perhaps be traced back to the messianic passages of the Hebrew Bible that prophesy the glorification of the King of the Jews following His advent, and the permeation of His message throughout the world. Here is an example from Isaiah.

The riches of the sea will flow to you, the wealth of nations come to you; camels in throngs will cover you, and dromedaries of Midian and Ephah; everyone in Sheba will come, bringing gold and incense and singing the praise of the Lord.[4]

Psalms 72: 10-11, Jeremiah 6: 20, and Ezekiel 27: 22 are other examples of prophetic texts that can provide the context for the story of the three Magi.

The second chapter of Luke refers to Simeon, a Jewish holy man who is filled with the Holy Spirit and thus learns of the greatness of the infant Jesus.

> And behold, there was a man in Jerusalem, whose name was Simeon; and the same man was just and devout, waiting for the consolation of Israel: and the Holy Ghost was upon him. And it was revealed unto him by the Holy Ghost, that he should not see death, before he had seen the Lord's Christ.
>
> And he came by the Spirit into the temple; and when the parents brought in the child Jesus, to do for him after the custom of the law, then he took him up in his arms, and blessed God, and said,
>
> "Lord, now lettest thou thy servant depart in peace, according to thy word: for mine eyes have seen thy salvation, which thou hast prepared before the face of all people; a light to lighten the Gentiles, and the glory of thy people Israel." And Joseph and his mother marvelled at those things which were spoken of him. And Simeon blessed them, and said unto Mary his mother, "Behold, this child is set for the fall and rising of many in Israel . . ."[5]

Islam

Muslim accounts of the life of Muhammad relate the story of Bahírá, a Christian monk who after studying a certain Christian sacred text concludes that he will soon behold a holy child bearing certain signs, chosen by God to lead his people. Bahírá lives in a monastery cell in Busra, Syria, near a caravan route used by the Arabs. One day, a caravan that includes the young Muhammad and His uncle Abú Tálib passes by Bahírá's monastery and the monk sees his wish fulfilled.

Abú Tálib had planned to go in a merchant caravan to Syria, and when all preparations had been made for the journey, the apostle of God [Muhammad], so they allege, attached himself closely to him so that he took pity on him and said that he would take him with him . . . When the caravan reached Búsrá in Syria, there was a monk there in his cell by the name of Bahírá, who was well versed in the knowledge of Christians. There he gained his knowledge from a book that was in the cell, so they allege, handed on from generation to generation. They had often passed by him in the past and he never spoke to them or took any notice of them until this year, and when they stopped near his cell he made a great feast for them.

It is alleged that that was because of something he saw while in his cell. They allege that while he was in his cell he saw the apostle of God in the caravan when they approached, with a cloud overshadowing him among the people . . . When Bahírá saw that, he came out of his cell and sent word to them, "I have prepared food for you . . ." One of them said to him, By God, Bahírá! something extraordinary has happened today, you used not to treat us so, and we have often passed by you . . . So they gathered together with him, leaving the apostle of God behind with the baggage under the tree, on account of his extreme youth . . . he [Bahírá] told them to invite him to come to the meal with them . . . When Bahírá saw him he stared at him closely, looking at his body and finding traces of his description (in the Christian books) . . . he began to ask him about what happened in his waking and his sleep, and his habits, and his affairs generally, and what the apostle of God told him coincided with what Bahírá knew of his description.

Then he looked at his back and saw the seal of prophethood between his shoulders in the very place

> described in his book. When he had finished he went to his uncle Abú Tálib and said ... "Take your nephew back to his country and guard him carefully against the Jews, for by Allah! if they see him and know about him what I know, they will do him evil; a great future lies before this nephew of yours, so take him home quickly."[6]

The Bahá'í Faith

Bahá'í accounts relate that during the childhood of Bahá'u'lláh, His father (a Persian nobleman and minister of State) has a strange dream about Him. Confused by what he has seen in the dream, he calls in a soothsayer, who explains that the child has a turbulent but glorious life ahead of Him.

> When Bahá'u'lláh was still a child, the Vazír, His father, dreamed a dream. Bahá'u'lláh appeared to him swimming in a vast, limitless ocean. His body shone upon the waters with a radiance that illumined the sea. Around His head, which could distinctly be seen above the waters, there radiated, in all directions, His long, jet-black locks, floating in great profusion above the waves. As he dreamed, a multitude of fishes gathered round Him, each holding fast to the extremity of one hair. Fascinated by the effulgence of His face, they followed Him in whatever direction He swam. Great as was their number, and however firmly they clung to His locks, not one single hair seemed to have been detached from His head, nor did the least injury affect His person. Free and unrestrained, He moved above the waters and they all followed Him.
>
> The Vazír, greatly impressed by this dream, summoned a soothsayer, who had achieved fame in that region, and asked him to interpret it for him. This man, as if inspired by a premonition of the future glory

of Bahá'u'lláh, declared: "The limitless ocean that you have seen in your dream, O Vazír, is none other than the world of being. Single-handed and alone, your son will achieve supreme ascendancy over it. Wherever He may please, He will proceed unhindered. No one will resist His march, no one will hinder His progress. The multitude of fishes signifies the turmoil which He will arouse amidst the peoples and kindreds of the earth. Around Him will they gather, and to Him will they cling. Assured of the unfailing protection of the Almighty, this tumult will never harm His person, nor will His loneliness upon the sea of life endanger His safety."

That soothsayer was subsequently taken to see Bahá'u'lláh. He looked intently upon His face, and examined carefully His features. He was charmed by His appearance, and extolled every trait of His countenance. Every expression in that face revealed to his eyes a sign of His concealed glory. So great was his admiration, and so profuse his praise of Bahá'u'lláh, that the Vazír, from that day, became even more passionately devoted to his son. The words spoken by that soothsayer served to fortify his hopes and confidence in Him. Like Jacob, he desired only to ensure the welfare of his beloved Joseph, and to surround Him with his loving protection.[7]

Struggles in Solitude

At a critical juncture in their lives, the founders of all the great religions go through a period of solitude in the course of which they often have to endure hardships or internal struggles with doubts, evil suggestions, or even demonic forces. By engaging in these internal battles and eventually conquering the enemy of self, ego, and passion variably depicted as Satan, demonic forces, or doubts, the Prophets provide distinct examples of steadfastness in the face of adversity.

Zoroaster

Rejected by family and foe alike, Zoroaster begins to doubt He will ever be the recipient of God's favor.

> To what land shall I flee? Where bend my steps?
> I am thrust out from family and tribe;
> I have no favour from the village to which I would belong,
> Nor from the wicked rulers of the country:
> How then, O Lord, shall I obtain thy favour? [1]

Zoroaster engages in battles with Angra Mainyu, the manifestation of evil. Neither threats of destruction nor promises of rewards from Angra Mainyu can persuade the righteous Zoroaster to turn away from his Lord (Ahura Mazda) and give allegiance to the devil.

> Angra Mainyu [Satan] sends the demon Buiti to kill Zarathustra; Zarathustra sings aloud the Ahuna-Vairya,

and the demon flies away, confounded by the sacred words and by the Glory of Zarathustra. Angra Mainyu himself attacks him and propounds riddles to be solved under pain of death. The Prophet rejects him with heavenly stones, given by Ahura, and announces to him that He will destroy his creation. The demon promises him the empire of the world if He adores him, as his ancestors have done, and abjures the religion of Mazda. Zarathustra rejects his offers scornfully. He announces He will destroy him with the arms given by Ahura, namely, the sacrificial implements and the sacred words. Then He recites the . . . Gatha in which He asks Ahura for instruction on all the mysteries of the material and spiritual world.[2]

Moses

When God informs Moses that He has chosen Him to lead the release of the Hebrews out of the yoke of Egyptian bondage, Moses expresses doubt and questions the Lord's judgment.

> And Moses said unto God, "Who am I, that I should go unto Pharaoh, and that I should bring forth the children of Israel out of Egypt?"[3]

When God tries to reassure Moses that He is the right person for this mission and that God will be there to assist Him throughout, a skeptical Moses still asks the Lord to choose someone else for the assignment.

> Now therefore go, and I will be with your mouth and teach you what you shall speak. But he [Moses] said, "Oh, my Lord, send I pray, some other person."[4]

Buddha

The young Buddha decides to leave His life of luxury behind and assume the mantle of asceticism in the hope of solving the riddle of life.

> The ascetic Gotama, while youthful, a black-haired youth, in the prime of his young days, in the first stage of life went forth from the household life to homelessness. Leaving his grieving parents weeping with tear-stained faces, having cut off his hair and beard and put on yellow robes, he went forth into homelessness.[5]

Mara – the lord of the five desires and the personification of evil in Buddhism – plots to prevent the Buddha from achieving enlightenment. He uses every weapon in his arsenal to distract the youthful Gautama, yet ultimately fails.

> The Holy One directed his steps to that blessed Bodhi-tree beneath whose shade he was to accomplish his search. As he walked, the earth shook and a brilliant light transfigured the world. When he sat down the heavens resounded with joy and all living beings were filled with good cheer. Mara alone, lord of the five desires, bringer of death and enemy of truth, was grieved and rejoiced not. With his three daughters, Tanha, Raga and Arati, the tempters, and with his host of evil demons, he went to the place where the great samana sat. But Sakyamuni heeded him not.
>
> Mara uttered fear-inspiring threats and raised a whirlwind so that the skies were darkened and the ocean roared and trembled. But the Blessed One under the Bodhi-tree remained calm and feared not. The Enlightened One knew that no harm could befall him. The three daughters of Mara tempted the Bodhisatta, but

he paid no attention to them, and when Mara saw that he could kindle no desire in the heart of the victorious samana, he ordered all the evil spirits at his command to attack him and overawe the great muni.

But the Blessed One watched them as one would watch the harmless games of children. All the fierce hatred of the evil spirits was of no avail. The flames of hell became wholesome breezes of perfume, and the angry thunderbolts were changed into lotus-blossoms.

When Mara saw this, he fled away with his army from the Bodhi-tree, whilst from above a rain of heavenly flowers fell, and voices of good spirits were heard:

"Behold the great muni! His heart unmoved by hatred. The wicked Mara's host against him did not prevail. Pure is he and wise, loving and full of mercy. As the rays of the sun drown the darkness of the world, so he who perseveres in his search will find the truth and the truth will enlighten him." [6]

Jesus

Shortly after the personification of the Spirit of God descends upon Jesus in the form of a dove, He sets out for the wilderness of Judea where He fasts and is tempted by the devil for forty days and nights.

And Jesus, full of the Holy Spirit, returned from the Jordan, and was led by the Spirit for forty days in the wilderness, tempted by the devil. And he ate nothing in those days; and when they were ended, he was hungry. The devil said to him, "If you are the Son of God, command this stone to become bread." And Jesus answered him, "It is written, 'Man shall not live by bread alone.'" And the devil took him up, and showed him all the kingdoms of the world in a moment of time, and said to him, "To you I will give all this authority and their glory; for it has been delivered to me, and I give it to whom I will. If you, then, will worship me, it shall all be yours." And Jesus answered him, "It is written, 'You shall worship the Lord your God, and him only shall you serve.'" And he took him to Jerusalem, and set him on the pinnacle of the temple, and said to him, "If you are the Son of God, throw yourself down from here; for it is written, 'He will give his angels charge of you, to guard you', and 'On their hands they will bear you up, lest you strike your foot against a stone.'" And Jesus answered him, "It is said, 'You shall not tempt the Lord your God.'" And when the devil had ended every temptation, he departed from him until an opportune time.[7]

Muhammad

Prior to receiving revelation, Muhammad often secludes Himself in a cave on Mount Hira, where He engages in deep contemplation of life and the many ills of His society, and in worshipping the one true God.

The commencement of the Divine Inspiration to Allah's Apostle was in the form of good dreams which came true like bright day light, and then the love of seclusion was bestowed upon him. He used to go in seclusion in the cave of Hira where he used to worship (Allah alone) continuously for many days before his desire to see his family. He used to take with him the journey food for the stay and then come back to (his wife) Khadija to take his food like-wise again till suddenly the Truth descended upon him while he was in the cave of Hira. The angel came to him and asked him to read.[8]

The Qur'án confirms that all Prophets have been tempted by Satan so that they can set an example for their followers on how to overcome evil.

> We have not sent any apostle or prophet before thee, among whose desires Satan injected not some *wrong* desire, but God shall bring to nought that which Satan had suggested. Thus shall God affirm His revelation for God is knowing, wise! That He may make that which Satan had injected, a trial to those in whose heart is a disease, and whose hearts are hardened.[9]

The Qur'án also assures Muhammad of the authenticity of the revelations He is receiving.

> And if thou art in doubt as to what We have sent down to thee, inquire at those who have read the Scriptures before thee. Now hath the truth come unto thee from thy Lord: be not therefore of those who doubt.[10]

Bahá'u'lláh

Bahá'í accounts relate that when Bahá'u'lláh faces opposition from His half-brother in attempting to regenerate the demoralized Bábí community of Iraq, He decides to leave Baghdad for the mountains of Kurdistan. There, for about a year, He lives the life of a virtual hermit before sojourning to a small town in the area for another year.

> Soon after Our arrival, We betook Ourself to the mountains of Kurdistán, where We led for a time a life of complete solitude. We sought shelter upon the summit of a remote mountain which lay at some three days' distance from the nearest human habitation. The comforts of life were completely lacking. We remained entirely

> isolated from Our fellow men until a certain Shaykh Ismá'íl discovered Our abode and brought Us the food We needed.[11]

These trials, while physically and emotionally challenging, appear to galvanize the spirit of Bahá'u'lláh and prepare Him for the future sufferings and persecution in store for Him and His family.

> In the early days of Our arrival in this land, when We discerned the signs of impending events, We decided, ere they happened, to retire. We betook Ourselves to the wilderness, and there, separated and alone, led for two years a life of complete solitude. From Our eyes there rained tears of anguish, and in Our bleeding heart there surged an ocean of agonizing pain. Many a night We had no food for sustenance, and many a day Our body found no rest.
>
> By Him Who hath My being between His hands! notwithstanding these showers of afflictions and unceasing calamities, Our soul was wrapt in blissful joy, and Our whole being evinced an ineffable gladness. For in Our solitude We were unaware of the harm or benefit, the health or ailment, of any soul. Alone, We communed with Our spirit, oblivious of the world and all that is therein.[12]

Prophetic Call

In the lives of the divine educators, there seems to be a momentous event signaling the beginning of their active ministries. It is through this initiatory event that they are awakened to their special mission – the guidance of their fellow human beings.

Buddha

The Buddha receives enlightenment under the sacred Bodhi tree.

> The Holy One directed his steps to that blessed Bodhi-tree beneath whose shade he was to accomplish his search. As he walked, the earth shook and a brilliant light transfigured the world. When he sat down the heavens resounded with joy and all living beings were filled with cheer.[1]

Zoroaster

After a ten-year seclusion, Zoroaster at the age of 30 has a vision in which He has an encounter with the archangel of Good Thought (Vohu Mana) who leads His soul into the presence of God, the Wise Lord or Ahura Mazda. Here, Zoroaster describes His encounter with the Wise Lord who entrusts Him with His mission:

> As the holy one I recognized thee, O Wise Lord,
> When he came to me as Good Mind and asked me:
> "Who art thou, whose art thou? Shall I appoint by a
> sign

The days when inquiry shall be made about thy living
possessions
and thyself?"

I made answer to him: "I am Zarathustra, first,
A true enemy to the wicked with all my might,
But a powerful support for the righteous,
So that I may attain the future blessings of the absolute
Dominion
By praising and singing thee, O Wise One!"

As the holy one I recognized thee, O Wise Lord,
When he came to me as Good Mind.
To his question: "To whom wilt thou address thy worship?"
I made reply: "To thy fire! While I offer up my veneration to it,
I will think of the Right to the utmost of my power."

As the holy one I recognized thee, O Wise Lord,
When he came to me as Good Mind;
The Silent Thought taught me the greatest good
So that I might proclaim it.
Let no man favour the many wicked,

For they make enemies of all righteous men.[2]

Moses

While shepherding a flock, Moses goes to the Mountain of God and receives the divine call from an angel of the Lord who appears in a bush that burns but is not consumed.

Now Moses was keeping the flock of his father-in-law, Jethro, the priest of Midian; and he led his flock to the west side of the wilderness, and came to Horeb, the mountain of God. And the angel of the Lord appeared to him in flame of fire out of the midst of a bush; and he looked, and lo, the bush was burning, yet it was not consumed. And Moses said, "I will turn aside and see this great sight, why the bush is not burnt." When the Lord saw that he turned aside to see, God called to him out of the bush, "Moses, Moses!" And he said, "Here am I!" Then he said, "Do not come near; put off your shoes from your feet, for the place on which you are standing is holy ground." And he said, "I am the God of your father, the God of Abraham, the God of Isaac, and the God of Jacob." And Moses hid his face, for he was afraid to look at God.

Then the Lord said, "I have seen the affliction of my people who are in Egypt, and have heard their cry because of their taskmasters; I know their sufferings, and I have come down to deliver them out of the hand of the Egyptians, and to bring them up to that land to a good and broad land, a land flowing with milk and honey, to the place of the Canaanites, the Hittites, the Amorites, the Perizzites, the Hivites, and the Jebusites. And now, behold, the cry of the people of Israel has come to me, and I have seen the oppression with which the Egyptians oppress them. Come, I will send you to Pharaoh that you may bring forth my people, the sons of Israel, out of Egypt." But Moses said to God, "Who am I that I should go to Pharaoh, and bring the sons of Israel out of Egypt?" He said, "But I will be with you; and this shall be the sign for you, that I have sent you: when you have brought forth the people out of Egypt, you shall serve God upon this mountain." [3]

Jesus

John the Baptist reluctantly baptizes Jesus. Soon, the Holy Spirit, personified in the form of a dove, descends upon Jesus.

> Then Jesus came from Galilee to the Jordan to John, to be baptized by him. John would have prevented him, saying, "I need to be baptized by you, and do you come to me?" But Jesus answered him, "Let it be so now; for thus it is fitting for us to fulfil all righteousness." Then he consented. And when Jesus was baptized, he went up immediately from the water, and behold, the heavens were opened and he saw the Spirit of God descending like a dove, and alighting on him; and lo, a voice from heaven, saying, "This is my beloved Son, with whom I am well pleased.[4]

Muhammad

Islamic tradition maintains that the entire Qur'án was revealed to Muhammad's soul during a certain night known as the Night of Power or Destiny (Laylat al-Qadr) in the month of Ramadan of the year 610 C.E. Then, over a 23-year period, the Prophet gradually revealed the verses to His followers on different occasions.

> Verily, We have caused It to descend on the night of Power.
> And who shall teach thee what the night of power is?
> The night of power excelleth a thousand months:
> Therein descend the angels and the spirit by permission of their Lord for every matter;
> And all is peace till the breaking of the morn.[5]

Muhammad has His first encounter with the divine presence, appearing in the form of the Archangel Gabriel who commands

Muhammad to recite. The terrified Muhammad prostrates Himself to the ground and asks "What shall I recite?" And the answer comes.

> Recite thou, in the name of thy Lord who created;-
> Created man from CLOTS OF BLOOD:-
> Recite thou! For thy Lord is the most beneficent,
> Who hath taught the use of the pen;-
> Hath taught man that which he knoweth not.[6]

Bahá'u'lláh

Bahá'u'lláh recollects His initial experiences of the divine as He lay in chains in the Black Pit, a dungeon in Tehran.

> While engulfed in tribulations I heard a most wondrous, a most sweet voice, calling above My head. Turning My face, I beheld a Maiden – the embodiment of the remembrance of the name of My Lord – suspended in the air before Me. So rejoiced was she in her very soul that her countenance shone with the ornament of the good pleasure of God, and her cheeks glowed with the brightness of the All-Merciful. Betwixt earth and heaven she was raising a call which captivated the hearts and minds of men. She was imparting to both My inward and outer being tidings which rejoiced My soul, and the souls of God's honored servants.
>
> Pointing with her finger unto My head, she addressed all who are in heaven and all who are on earth, saying: "By God! This is the Best-Beloved of the worlds, and yet ye comprehend not. This is the Beauty of God amongst you, and the power of His sovereignty within you, could ye but understand. This is the Mystery of God and His Treasure, the Cause of God and His glory unto all who are in the kingdoms of Revelation and of creation, if ye

be of them that perceive. This is He Whose Presence is the ardent desire of the denizens of the Realm of eternity, and of them that dwell within the Tabernacle of glory, and yet from His beauty do ye turn aside."[7]

In other works, Bahá'u'lláh reiterates how His mystical experiences of the divine have transformed and prepared Him for His perilous mission.

O King! I was but a man like others, asleep upon My couch, when lo, the breezes of the All-Glorious were wafted over Me, and taught Me the knowledge of all that hath been. This thing is not from Me, but from One Who is Almighty and All-Knowing. And He bade Me lift up My voice between earth and heaven, and for this there befell Me what hath caused the tears of every man of understanding to flow. The learning current amongst men I studied not; their schools I entered not. Ask of the city wherein I dwelt, that thou mayest be well assured that I am not of them who speak falsely. This is but a leaf which the winds of the will of thy Lord, the Almighty, the All-Praised, have stirred. Can it be still when the tempestuous winds are blowing? Nay, by Him Who is the Lord of all Names and Attributes! They move it as they list. The evanescent is as nothing before Him Who is the Ever-Abiding. His all-compelling summons hath reached Me, and caused Me to speak His praise amidst all people. I was indeed as one dead when His behest was uttered. The hand of the will of thy Lord, the Compassionate, the Merciful, transformed Me.[8]

God is My witness, O people! I was asleep on My couch, when lo, the Breeze of God wafting over Me roused Me from My slumber. His quickening Spirit revived Me, and My tongue was unloosed to voice His Call. Accuse

Me not of having transgressed against God. Behold Me, not with your eyes but with Mine. Thus admonisheth you He Who is the Gracious, the All-Knowing. Think ye, O people, that I hold within My grasp the control of God's ultimate Will and Purpose? Far be it from Me to advance such claim. To this I testify before God, the Almighty, the Exalted, the All-Knowing, the All-Wise. Had the ultimate destiny of God's Faith been in Mine hands, I would have never consented, even though for one moment, to manifest Myself unto you, nor would I have allowed one word to fall from My lips. Of this God Himself is, verily, a witness.[9]

Their Dual Nature

The exact nature and station of the divine educators has long been a source of debate. Disagreements over the issue of whether they are primarily divine or human, or of a dual nature, have resulted in sectarianism, violence, and bloodshed among the masses of the faithful. The early history of Christianity offers a good example of this in the well-known Arian controversy.

Arius, a learned priest of Alexandria in Egypt, argued that Christ, as the Son, was a creation of the Father and therefore a finite being, mortal like others. To him, the appellation "Son of God" in the Gospels was simply a mark of respect for Jesus, not an indication of divine incarnation. Thousands of Christians found Arius' arguments convincing and joined ranks with him. Though he was excommunicated for his unorthodox views, Arius and his followers held firm in their beliefs and spread their teachings far and wide. Soon Constantine, the first Christian convert among Roman Emperors, who wanted to preserve the unity of his empire, held the first of a series of ecumenical councils of the Church at Nicaea, across the Bosphorus from Constantinople (Istanbul). There, after much debate over the true nature of Christ, it was proclaimed that Jesus was consubstantial (one in essence) with the Father.

This announcement, far from bringing peace and unity among Christians, led to a conflict that raged for over 50 years. Christians fought each other in the streets over the proper understanding of the nature of Christ. Thousands were killed. Eventually, Arius and his now mutilated party were defeated and the Christology of the Church Fathers led to the formation and adoption of the notion of Trinity: the Father, the Son, and the Holy Ghost were all consubstantial, three beings in one. Jesus, in parallel with the Greek philosophical concept of Logos, became the agent of creation. He also came to be considered the full incarnation of God in the flesh.

Today, contemporary Christianity continues to view Jesus as primarily divine in nature and one in essence with the Father. Long before Christianity, though, many strands of Hinduism had developed the same understanding of the reality of their holy figures. Worshippers of the various Hindu deities such as Vishnu, Shiva, Brahma, and Krishna have for centuries considered these personages to be superhuman devas with divine qualities and powers and as agents of the creation, preservation, and destruction of the universe.

At the opposite end of the spectrum are the orthodox traditions of Judaism, Islam, and Theravada Buddhism, which regard Moses, Muhammad, and Buddha as mortals with divine missions or, in the case of Buddha, simply as wise and enlightened souls with magnetic personalities. Interestingly, both these extreme views find support in the sacred literature of all the different religious traditions. Certain passages validate the mortality of the founders and present them as individuals subjected to the same needs, limitations, and emotions as the rest of us, while other passages point to a higher nature that places them above the realm of humanity and endows them with a unique capacity to receive revelation and enlightenment from a higher source. The deeds and words of these holy personages are proclaimed as divine in nature and thus capable of providing unfailing guidance and spiritual protection to others.

The Bahá'í Faith affirms that the founders of the religions have two natures – divine and human. In their divine aspect, it considers them as sharing in one and the same reality. Bahá'u'lláh calls this the station of the unity of the Prophets. Yet, like the rest of us, they too have their own distinct personalities and individual souls, which establish their humanness. Bahá'u'lláh calls this second aspect the station of "distinction." Unlike the station of unity, where they manifest God's grandeur and sovereignty to humanity, in the station of distinction they provide perfect examples of servitude to God so that we can emulate them.

> The other is the station of distinction, and pertaineth to the world of creation and to the limitations thereof. In this respect, each Manifestation of God hath a distinct individuality, a definitely prescribed mission, a predestined Revelation, and specially designated limitations. Each one of them is known by a different name, is characterized by a special attribute, fulfils a definite Mission, and is entrusted with a particular Revelation . . . Viewed in the light of their second station – the station of distinction, differentiation, temporal limitations, characteristics and standards – they manifest absolute servitude, utter destitution and complete self-effacement.[1]

Their Divine Nature

Krishna

The Bhagavad Gita is full of references by Krishna to His divine nature.

> But beyond my visible nature is my invisible Spirit. This is the fountain of life whereby this universe has its being.[2]

> The unwise think that I am that form of my lower nature which is seen by mortal eyes: they know not my higher nature, imperishable and supreme.[3]

> For my glory is not seen by all: I am hidden by my veil of mystery; and in its delusion the world knows me not, who was never born and for ever I am. I know all that was and is and is to come, Arjuna; but no one in truth knows me.[4]

> But there are some great souls who know me: their refuge is my own divine nature. They love me with a oneness of love: they know that I am the source of all.[5]
>
> He who knows I am beginningless, unborn, the Lord of all the worlds, this mortal is free from delusion, and from all evils he is free.[6]
>
> Of sounds I am the first sound, A; of compounds I am coordination. I am time, never-ending time. I am the Creator who sees all.[7]
>
> There is no end of my divine greatness, Arjuna. What I have spoken here to thee shows only a small part of my Infinity.[8]

Buddha

Buddha identifies His nature with that of the Norm (Divine Person).

> He who sees the Norm, he sees me; he who sees me, he sees the Norm.[9]

Buddha claims not only that He knows the Brahma (Creator) world but that He was born within it, an allusion to His divine nature.

> If a man had been born and brought up in [the town of] Manasakata, every road that leads to Manasakata would be perfectly familiar to him . . . to the Tathagata,* when asked touching the path which leads to the world of Brahma, there can be no doubt of difficulty. For

* He who exemplifies his own teachings.

> Brahma, I know, Vasettha [a Brahmin], and the world of Brahma, and the path which leadeth unto it. Yea, I know it even as one who has entered the Brahma world, and has been born within it![10]

Buddha states that the reality or inner essence of a Tathagata is unknowable.

> Since a Tathagata, even when actually present, is incomprehensible, it is inept to say of him – the Uttermost Person, the Supernal Person, the Attainer of the Supernal; that after dying the Tathagata is, or is not, or both is and is not, or neither is nor is not.[11]

Buddha affirms that His true nature is beyond this world and has overcome it.

> Dona [a Brahmin] approached the Lord and said:
> "Is your reverence a god?"
> "No indeed, Brahmin, I am not a god."
> "Then an angel?"
> "No indeed, Brahmin."
> "A fairy, then?"
> "No indeed, Brahmin, I am not a fairy."
> "Then is your reverence a human being?"
> "No indeed, Brahmin, I am not a human being."
> "You answer NO to all my questions. Who then is your reverence?"
> "Brahmin, those outflows whereby, if they had not been extinguished, I might have been a god, angel, fairy, or a human being – those outflows are extinguished in me, cut off at the root, make like a palm-tree stump that can come to no further existence in the future. Just as a blue, red, or white lotus, although born in the water, grown up in the water, when it reaches the

> surface stands there unsoiled by the water – just so, Brahmin, although born in the world, grown up in the world, having overcome the world, I abide unsoiled by the world. Take it that I am Buddha."[12]

Moses

Moses identifies himself with God.

> And Moses summoned all Israel and said to them: . . . "I have led you forty years in the wilderness; your clothes have not worn out upon you, and your sandals have not worn off your feet; you have not eaten bread, and you have not drunk wine or strong drink; that you may know that I am the Lord your God."[13]

God tells Moses that He shall be as God to Aaron in their dealings with the Israelites.

> He [Aaron] shall speak for you [Moses] to the people; and he shall be a mouth for you, and you shall be to him as God.[14]

In their encounter with the Pharaoh, God compares the role of Moses to Himself (divinity) and that of Aaron to Moses (prophethood).

> And the LORD said to Moses, "See, I make you as God to Pharaoh; and Aaron your brother shall be your prophet."[15]

The following passage confirms both the human (servitude) and divine nature of Moses; someone with a higher station than the other Hebrew prophets (those with only visions of God).

And he [God] said, "Hear my words: If there is a prophet among you, I the Lord make myself known to him in a vision, I speak with him in a dream. Not so with my servant Moses; he is entrusted with all my house. With him I speak mouth to mouth, clearly, and not in dark speech; and he beholds the form of the Lord. Why then were you not afraid to speak against my servant Moses?"[16]

Jesus

Jesus refers to the eternal nature of His reality (inner self).

Jesus said to them, "Truly, truly, I say to you, before Abraham was, I am."[17]

I am the Alpha and the Omega, the beginning and the end.[18]

Father, glorify thou me in thy own presence with the glory which I had with thee before the world was made.[19]

He confirms His divine nature on numerous occasions.

I and the Father are one.[20]

. . . the Father is in me and I am in the Father.[21]

If you had known me, you would have known my Father also; henceforth you know him and have seen him. Philip said to him, "Lord, show us the Father, and we shall be satisfied." Jesus said to him, "Have I been with you so long, and yet you do not know me, Philip? He who has seen me has seen the Father; How can you say, 'Show us the Father'? Do you not believe that I am

> in the Father and the Father in me?"[22]

> All that the Father has is mine.[23]

> . . . whoever receives me, receives not me but him who sent me.[24]

> In the beginning was the Word, and the Word was with God, and the Word was God. He was in the beginning with God; all things were made through him, and without him was not anything made that was made.[25]

Muhammad

God proclaims Muhammad's unity with Him.

> In truth, they who plighted fealty to thee, really plighted that fealty to God.[26]

> Whoso obeyeth the Apostle, in so doing obeyeth God.[27]

> Whoever sees me [Muhammad] has seen God.[28]

Muhammad confirms His dual natures of servitude (humanness) and divinity.

> Outwardly, we are the last of all, but inwardly we preceded everyone.[29]

Bahá'u'lláh

Bahá'u'lláh explicitly proclaims the higher nature (divinity) of the Prophets as manifestors of God's perfections and attributes (hence, Manifestations of God) in the world of existence.

> Were any of the all-embracing Manifestations of God to declare: "I am God!" He verily speaketh the truth, and no doubt attacheth thereto. For it hath been repeatedly demonstrated that through their Revelation, their attributes and names, the Revelation of God, His name and His attributes, are made manifest in the world.[30]

In the following passages, He becomes the conduit for God voicing His Oneness.

> . . . Verily, there is none other God but Me, the Everlasting, the Peerless, the Ancient of Days.[31]

> . . . Verily, no God is there but Me, the Powerful, the Mighty, the All-Subduing, the Most Exalted, the Omniscient, the All-Wise.[32]

Bahá'u'lláh explains that the Manifestations of God act as mirrors reflecting God's beauty to humankind.

> We recognize in the manifestation of each one of them, whether outwardly or inwardly, the manifestation of none but God Himself, if ye be of those that comprehend. Every one of them is a mirror of God, reflecting naught else but His Self, His Beauty, His Might and Glory, if ye will understand.[33]

Bahá'u'lláh equates the knowledge and recognition of the Manifestations of God with the knowledge and recognition of God Himself.

> The door of the knowledge of the Ancient Being hath ever been, and will continue for ever to be, closed in the face of men. No man's understanding shall ever gain access unto His holy court. As a token of His mercy,

however, and as a proof of His loving-kindness, He hath manifested unto men the Day Stars of His divine guidance, the Symbols of His divine unity, and hath ordained the knowledge of these sanctified Beings to be identical with the knowledge of His own Self.

Whoso recognizeth them hath recognized God. Whoso hearkeneth to their call, hath hearkened to the Voice of God, and whoso testifieth to the truth of their Revelation, hath testified to the truth of God Himself. Whoso turneth away from them, hath turned away from God, and whoso disbelieveth in them, hath disbelieved in God. Every one of them is the Way of God that connecteth this world with the realms above, and the Standard of His Truth unto every one in the kingdoms of earth and heaven. They are the Manifestations of God amidst men, the evidences of His Truth, and the signs of His glory.[34]

Their Human Nature

Krishna

Krishna states that some are fooled by His human side and fail to recognize His higher nature.

But the fools of the world know me not when they see me in my own human body. They know not my Spirit supreme, the Infinite God of this all.[35]

Prince Arjuna, Krishna's cousin and friend, realizes that Krishna, while having a human side, is in reality much more than His physical form.

If in careless presumption, or even in friendliness, I said "Krishna! Son of Yadu! My friend!", this I did unconscious of thy greatness. And if in irreverence I was disrespectful – when alone or with others – and made a jest of thee at games, or resting, or at a feast, forgive me in thy mercy, O thou Immeasurable.[36]

Moses

The Hebrew Bible notes that Moses, while a Prophet, was a very meek man.

Now the man Moses was very meek, more than all men that were on the face of the earth.[37]

Jesus

Jesus asserts that He is an agent of God the Father, who is much greater than Him.

All things have been delivered to me by my Father.[38]

And Jesus said to him, "Why do you call me good? No one is good but God alone."[39]

. . . I seek not my own will but the will of him who sent me.[40]

So Jesus answered them, "My teaching is not mine, but his who sent me."[41]

. . . and that I do nothing on my own authority but speak thus as the Father taught me. And he who sent me is with me; he has not left me alone, for I always do what is pleasing to Him.[42]

. . . I came not of my own accord, but he sent me.[43]

> For I have not spoken on my own authority; the Father who sent me has himself given me commandment what to say and what to speak. And I know that his commandment is eternal life. What I say, therefore, I say as the Father has bidden me.[44]

> . . . the Father is greater than I.[45]

> I do as the Father has commanded me . . .[46]

> Jesus said to them, "Truly, truly, I say to you, the Son can do nothing of his own accord, but only what he sees the Father doing; for whatever he does, that the Son does likewise."[47]

The early Christians understood this aspect of Jesus' relationship to God.

> . . . Jesus of Nazareth, a man attested to you by God with mighty works and wonders and signs which God did through him in your midst . . .[48]

Jesus' contemporaries were baffled by His wisdom and greatness because they were solely focusing on His human side.

> And when Jesus had finished these parables, he went away from there, and coming to his own country he taught them in their synagogue, so that they were astonished, and said, "Where did this man get this wisdom and these mighty works? Is not this the carpenter's son? Is not his mother called Mary? And are not his brothers James and Joseph and Simon and Judas?"[49]

Muhammad

The Qur'án affirms that Muhammad is only a mortal like other humans.

> Say: "I am only a mortal the like of you . . ."[50]

It also states that Muhammad was nothing more than a messenger.

> Muhammad is no more than an apostle . . .[51]

Bahá'u'lláh

Bahá'u'lláh confesses His servitude to God.

> I am but a servant of God Who hath believed in Him and in His signs, and in His Prophets and in His angels. My tongue, and My heart, and My inner and My outer being testify that there is no God but Him, that all others have been created by His behest, and been fashioned through the operation of His Will.[52]

Bahá'u'lláh also clearly distinguishes between His two natures.

> Know verily that whenever this Youth [Bahá'u'lláh] turneth His eyes towards His own self, he findeth it the most insignificant of all creation. When He contemplates, however, the bright effulgences He hath been empowered to manifest, lo, that self is transfigured before Him into a sovereign Potency permeating the essence of all things visible and invisible.[53]

Their Unity

If these holy figures do indeed possess a divine nature, must they not all share in the same quintessential reality? A way to examine the validity of this assumption is to look for outer expressions of such an intangible reality in their daily lives. If we find the deeds, words, and aims of Krishna, Zoroaster, Moses, Jesus, Muhammad, Buddha, and Bahá'u'lláh to be in essential harmony, it is probably safe to assume that they all do indeed share in the same inner reality. A close study of the characters of these figures appears to corroborate this. For instance, we see that each and every one of them has manifested, throughout His earthly life, those same attributes we normally associate with the divine, such as love, compassion, forgiveness, and generosity. The driving motives behind their missions also seem to have been identical – the spiritualization of mankind and the improvement of the human condition.

Thus, much like different teachers in an elementary school who receive the same general mandate (to educate the child) from the same Principal, these holy figures seem to have had the same general mission (the guidance of humanity) and have been commissioned by the same Divine Principal (God). While maintaining their distinct personalities and individual souls, they appear to have been animated by the same great Spirit.

In this regard, Bahá'u'lláh's use of the analogy of the sun and the mirrors may again prove helpful.

> These sanctified Mirrors, these Day Springs of ancient glory, are, one and all, the Exponents on earth of Him Who is the central Orb of the universe, its Essence and ultimate Purpose. From Him proceed their knowledge

> and power; from Him is derived their sovereignty . . . By the revelation of these Gems of Divine virtue all the names and attributes of God, such as knowledge and power, sovereignty and dominion, mercy and wisdom, glory, bounty, and grace, are made manifest.[1]

Thus, God is likened to the sun and the divine educators to mirrors reflecting the rays of the sun. Just as the physical sun supports various life forms on earth through heat, light, and energy, the spiritual Sun (God) supports the existence and development of the human soul by sending the rays of His perfections to humanity through the founders of the religions. By reflecting the rays of the spiritual Sun from themselves, the divine mirrors carry the life-giving warmth and energy of that Sun to the soul of humankind. The mirrors are many but the spiritual Sun (God) reflected in the mirrors is one and the same.

Buddha

Buddha affirms the oneness of the divine educators and the unity of their purpose.

> There is no distinction between any of the Buddhas in physical beauty, moral habit, concentration, wisdom, cognition and insight of freedom, the four confidences, the ten powers of a Tathagata, the six special cognitions, the fourteen cognitions of Buddhas, eighteen Buddha-dhammas, in a word in all the dhamma of Buddhas, for all Buddhas are exactly the same as regards Buddha-dhammas.[2]

Jesus

Jesus confirms His oneness with the divine educators of past and future.

> I am the Alpha and the Omega, the beginning and the end.[3]

> If you believed Moses, you would believe me, for he wrote of me. But if you do not believe his writings, how will you believe my words?[4]

Christ also announced the spiritual oneness of Elijah and John the Baptist.

> But I tell you that Elijah has already come, and they did not know him, but did to him whatever they pleased . . . Then the disciples understood that he was speaking to them of John the Baptist.[5]

Jesus testifies that the divine educator who comes after Him – the Counselor – will confirm His mission and teachings.

> But when the Counselor comes, whom I shall send to you from the Father, even the Spirit of truth, who proceeds from the Father, he will bear witness to me; and you also are witnesses, because you have been with me from the beginning.[6]

Muhammad

The Qur'án treats all Prophets as equals.

> Say ye: "We believe in God, and that which hath been sent down to us, and that which hath been sent down to Abraham and Ismael, and Isaac and Jacob and the tribes: and that which hath been given to Moses and to Jesus, and that which was given to the prophets from their Lord. No difference do we make between any of them . . .[7]

And they who believe on God and His apostles, and make no difference between them – these! We will bestow on them their reward at last. God is gracious, merciful.[8]

The Qur'án also confirms that the fundamental teachings of all the divine educators are the same.

Nothing hath been said to thee [Muhammad] which hath not been said of old to apostles before thee . . .[9]

Of a truth they who believe not on God and His apostles, and seek to separate God from His apostles, and say, "Some we believe, and some we believe not," and desire to take a middle way; These! They are veritable infidels! And for the infidels have We prepared a shameful punishment.[10]

Bahá'u'lláh

Bahá'u'lláh proclaims that all the Prophets are one and the same in essence.

Know thou assuredly that the essence of all the Prophets of God is one and the same. Their unity is absolute. God, the Creator, saith: There is no distinction whatsoever among the Bearers of My Message. They all have but one purpose; their secret is the same secret. To prefer one in honor to another, to exalt certain ones above the rest, is in no wise to be permitted. Every true Prophet hath regarded His Message as fundamentally the same as the Revelation of every other Prophet gone before Him.[11]

Bahá'u'lláh bears witness to the equal station of all the Prophets.

These attributes of God are not, and have never been, vouchsafed specially unto certain Prophets, and withheld from others . . . That a certain attribute of God hath not been outwardly manifested by these Essences of Detachment doth in no wise imply that they who are the Day Springs of God's attributes and the Treasuries of His holy names did not actually possess it.[12]

Beware, O believers in the Unity of God, lest ye be tempted to make any distinction between any of the Manifestations of His Cause, or to discriminate against the signs that have accompanied and proclaimed their Revelation . . . Whoso maketh the slightest possible difference between their persons, their words, their messages, their acts and manners, hath indeed disbelieved in God, hath repudiated His signs, and betrayed the Cause of His Messengers.[13]

It is clear and evident to thee that all the Prophets are the Temples of the Cause of God, Who have appeared clothed in divers attire. If thou wilt observe with discriminating eyes, thou wilt behold them all abiding in the same tabernacle, soaring in the same heaven, seated upon the same throne, uttering the same speech, and proclaiming the same Faith. Such is the unity of those Essences of being, those Luminaries of infinite and immeasurable splendour. Wherefore, should one of these Manifestations of Holiness proclaim saying: "I am the return of all the Prophets," He verily speaketh the truth.[14]

Revealers of Truth

A central goal of religion is transformation of human character. The means for bringing this about are the teachings that the founders of different religions – the divine educators – bring us. Collectively, these teachings constitute the "Truth" or the "Path." Followers accept the divine origin and transformative power of these teachings and adopt and practise them in their daily lives. By allowing these teachings to permeate their thoughts, deeds, and words, they can expect eventually to internalize and consistently manifest the same kind of nobility and virtuous character that their exemplars have shown.

Throughout history, all religious systems have emphasized the need to manifest noble virtues such as trustworthiness, love, truthfulness, unity, and detachment from worldly desires. Thus, over time, the consistent practice of these virtues has helped us as a species to rise to much higher stages of civilization. Religious education has played an undeniable role in this amazing metamorphosis of our species over centuries.

As exemplary leaders, the divine educators have not merely revealed and preached the Truth but have embodied it in their daily lives. They have not simply pointed to the Path; they have been the first to walk in it, and thus have provided an approachable model of behavior for us to emulate. By the dynamic force of their example, these holy figures have attempted to liberate humankind from the darkness of our lower nature and refocus our thoughts, words, and deeds on our higher nature.

Without this shift in focus, humanity tends to expend its energies on satisfying the needs of the body at the expense of the life of the soul. In the process, the materialistic person will take any measures, including sacrificing others, to satisfy his or her material or carnal desires. The life of the soul is gradually extinguished and the destructive characteristics of the person's lower nature begin to dominate. Religions try to revert this destructive process that can lead to the dehumanization and brutalization of the individual and result in chaos and turmoil in society.

Yet this "Truth" is revealed according to the exigencies of time and place. While their teachings are often radical enough to constitute a clear departure from existing traditions, all the founders of the religions have maintained continuity with the past by revealing these teachings in a language that is familiar and acceptable to those they are addressing. This has often meant resemblances to existing traditions in vocabulary, doctrine, theology, cosmology, and mythology.[1]

Thus we see that Buddha's message has clear Hindu underpinnings, Christ's teachings have a distinct Jewish base, and Muhammad's religion demonstrates obvious ties to Judeo-Christian and Zoroastrian traditions.

Interestingly, most of these holy figures appear to have claimed exclusive access to the Truth. Yet close scrutiny of their teachings seems to reveal that, in reality, these claims of exclusivity have not been intended to invalidate or trivialize the claims of other divine educators. Rather, they are to be understood within the context of the time and societies in which they were made. Within that framework, each holy figure may indeed be perceived as the only way to Truth for His time. In His own unique way, each divine educator has stood at the summit of Truth, unrivaled by any of His contemporaries. Thus, as the revealer of the highest and most recent form of Truth for His age, each divine educator has indeed been the one and only way to the Truth. Yet they do not engage in censuring their predecessors or proclaiming them to be imposters. On the contrary, we often see them glorifying those who came before them. For instance, we see Jesus reverencing Moses, Muhammad paying tribute to both Moses and Jesus, and

Bahá'u'lláh in His writings exalting all His predecessors, including specifically Zoroaster, Moses, Jesus and Muhammad.

Krishna

In the passage below, Krishna identifies two different paths to acquiring perfections – the path of wisdom and the path of action.

> In this world there are two roads of perfection, as I told thee before, O prince without sin [Arjuna]; Jnana Yoga, the path of wisdom of the Sankhyas, and Karma Yoga, the path of action of the Yogis.[2]

Krishna later identifies a third path: that of personal devotion to Him as the revealer and standard of Truth.

> And remembering me he utters OM, the eternal WORD of Brahman, he goes to the Path Supreme.[3]

Here, Krishna clearly warns that those who do not follow His Path are unwise, confused, and lost.

> Those who ever follow my doctrine and who have faith, and have a good will, find through pure work their freedom. But those who follow not my doctrine, and who have ill-will, are men blind to all wisdom, confused in mind; they are lost.[4]

Centuries before Christ, Krishna claims to be the creator of the universe, the beginning, the middle, and the end of all things, and the only way to the Truth.

> I am the Father of this universe, and even the Source of the Father. I am the Mother of this universe, and the Creator of all. I am the Highest to be known, the Path

of purification, the holy OM, the Three Vedas. I am the Way, and the Master who watches in silence; thy friend and thy shelter and thy abode of peace. I am the beginning and the middle and the end of all things: their seed of Eternity, their Treasure supreme.[5]

I am the beginning and the middle and the end of all that is. Of all knowledge I am the knowledge of the Soul. Of the many paths of reason I am the one that leads to Truth.[6]

Buddha

Buddha declares Himself the king of truth who has come for the salvation of the world.

I was born into the world as the king of truth for the salvation of the world.[7]

Buddha teaches that those who follow His example will become enlightened (knowers of His Path), will guide others to the Path, and display purified, holy lives.

He who goes for refuge to Buddha, to Truth and to those whom he taught, he goes indeed to a great refuge . . .[8]

. . . a Tathagata* arises in the world, an Arahant, fully-enlightened Buddha, endowed with wisdom and conduct, Well-Farer, Knower of the worlds, incomparable Trainer of men to be tamed, Teacher of gods and humans, enlightened and blessed . . . He preaches the Dhamma which is lovely in its beginning, lovely in its middle, lovely in its ending, in the spirit and in the letter, and displays the fully-perfected and purified holy life.[9]

---

* See note on page 25.

Like Krishna, in numerous passages Buddha identifies His Path as the best or only path to the Truth.

> The best of the paths is the path of eight [Buddha's Noble Eight-Fold Path]. The best of truths, the four sayings [Buddha's Four Noble Truths]. The best of states, freedom from passions. The best of men, the one who sees.
>
> This is the path. There is no other that leads to vision. Go on this path, and you will confuse MARA, the devil of confusion.
>
> Whoever goes on this path travels to the end of his sorrow. I showed this path to the world when I found the roots of sorrow.[10]

> The wise student shall find the Dhammapada [Path of Truth/Light], the clear Path of Perfection, even as a man who seeks flowers finds the most beautiful flowers.[11]

> Better than a hundred years not seeing the Path supreme is one single day of life if one sees the Path supreme.[12]

Zoroaster

Zoroaster declares Himself to be a Prophet and prays that the Wise Lord will continue to show His precepts to Him so he can preach them to humanity.

> To me, Zarathustra, the prophet and sworn friend of Righteousness,
> Lifting my voice with veneration, O Wise One,
> May the creator of the mind's force show, as Good Mind,
> His precepts, that they may be the path of my tongue.[13]

> . . . To whom will help come through the Good Mind?

To me, for I am chosen for the revelation by thee, O
Lord.[14]

Zoroaster asserts that His teachings reveal righteousness in the world and lead men to eternal bliss. Humans can attain the good pleasure of the Wise Lord (God) by manifesting righteous thoughts, words, and deeds in the world.

The best possession of Zarathustra Spitama[†] has been
revealed:
It is that the Wise Lord has granted, through the Right,
eternal bliss
To him and to all those who have observed and practised
The words and deeds of his good religion.[15]

By the thought of him, by words and deeds,
Shall prince Vistaspa and Spitama, Zarathustra's son,
And Frasaostra strive willingly
To please the Wise One and to pray in his praise,
Making even the paths to the religion of the saviour,
Which the Lord has ordained.[16]

(The Listeners:)
May he attain the best of the good,
He who teaches us the straight paths of salvation
– In this bodily existence and that of the Mind –
The true paths to those beings with whom the Lord
dwells,
The Lord which thou art, O Wise One, zealous, holy, of
fair race.[17]

Like other divine educators, Zoroaster claims His doctrines and teachings are the best.

---

† The family name of Zoroaster.

For the initiate, that is the best of the doctrines
Which the beneficent Lord teaches, as Righteousness, the Holy One which thou art,
Thou who knowest also, O Wise One,
Through the strength of Good Mind the secret doctrines.[18]

I will speak of the word which the Most Holy Wise Lord
Has told me as the best for mankind to hear:
"Those who for me shall give heed and obedience to him,
Shall attain integrity and Immortality through the deeds of Good Mind."[19]

Moses

God (Yahweh) reveals the core of His teachings to Moses on Mount Sinai, etched in stone tablets in the form of the Ten Commandments.

> The LORD said to Moses, "Come up to me on the mountain, and wait there; and I will give you the tables of stone, with the law and the commandment, which I have written for their instruction." So Moses rose with his servant Joshua, and Moses went up into the mountain of God . . . Then Moses went up on the mountain, and the cloud covered the mountain . . . Now the appearance of the glory of the LORD was like a devouring fire on the top of the mountain in the sight of the people of Israel. And Moses entered the cloud, and went up on the mountain. And Moses was on the mountain forty days and forty nights.[20]

The purpose of God in sending His laws to the children of Israel is to make them holy.

> And the LORD said to Moses, "Say to all the congregation of the people of Israel, You shall be holy; for I the LORD your God am holy."[21]

God assures the children of Israel that He will continue to dwell among them through the Ten Commandments. The purpose of this "dwelling" is to sanctify their characters.

> And I will dwell among the people of Israel, and will be their God. And they shall know that I am the LORD their God, who brought them forth out of the land of Egypt that I might dwell among them; I am the LORD their God.[22]

Jesus

Jesus reveals God the Father to humankind.

> No one has ever seen God; the only Son, who is in the bosom of the Father, he has made him known.[23]

Whoever denies Jesus the Son is also denying God the Father.

> Who is the liar but he who denies that Jesus is the Christ? This is the antichrist, he who denies the Father and the Son. No one who denies the Son has the Father. He who confesses the Son has the Father also.[24]

Jesus ushers in a new religion and, in the process, repeals several laws of the Mosaic dispensation.

> And he said to them, "The sabbath was made for man, not man for the sabbath; so the Son of man is lord even of the sabbath."[25]

> It was also said, "Whoever divorces his wife, let him give her a certificate of divorce." But I say to you that every one who divorces his wife, except on the ground of unchastity, makes her an adulteress; and whoever marries a divorced woman commits adultery.[26]

Jesus makes it clear that the requirements of His age are different from those in the time of Moses. A new, higher level of human conduct is set forth.

> You have heard that it was said, "An eye for an eye and a tooth for a tooth." But I say to you, Do not resist one who is evil. But if any one strikes you on the right cheek, turn to him the other also; and if any one would sue you and take your coat, let him have your cloak as well.[27]

> You have heard that it was said, "You shall love your neighbor and hate your enemy." But I say to you, Love your enemies and pray for those who persecute you, so that you may be sons of your Father who is in heaven; for he makes his sun rise on the evil and on the good, and sends rain on the just and on the unjust. For if you love those who love you, what reward have you?[28]

His followers must strive to be perfect, as their Father in heaven.

> You, therefore, must be perfect, as your heavenly Father is perfect.[29]

In the historic Sermon on the Mount, Jesus identifies the virtues of the blessed. These constitute the core of His teachings.

> Blessed are the meek, for they shall inherit the earth. Blessed are those who hunger and thirst for righteousness, for they shall be satisfied. Blessed are the merciful,

for they shall obtain mercy. Blessed are the pure in heart, for they shall see God. Blessed are the peacemakers, for they shall be called sons of God. Blessed are those who are persecuted for righteousness' sake, for theirs is the kingdom of heaven.

Blessed are you when men revile you and persecute you and utter all kinds of evil against you falsely on my account. Rejoice and be glad, for your reward is great in heaven, for so men persecuted the prophets who were before you.[30]

Several passages in the New Testament bear witness to the uniqueness of Christ and claim that human beings can find salvation only through Him.

Jesus said to him, "I am the way, and the truth, and the life; no one comes to the Father, but by me."[31]

And there is salvation in no one else, for there is no other name under heaven given among men by which we must be saved.[32]

I am the door; if any one enters by me, he will be saved, and will go in and out and find pasture.[33]

Muhammad

God establishes that Muhammad is His messenger, invites His servants to obey the Prophet if they desire to be guided to the straight path, and warns those who turn away from Him.

O Prophet ! we have sent thee to be a witness, and a herald of glad tidings, and a warner; And one who, through His own permission, summoneth to God, and a light-giving torch.[34]

> Say: Obey God and obey the Apostle. Suppose that ye turn back, still the burden of his duty is on him only, and the burden of your duty rests on you. If ye obey Him, ye shall have guidance: but plain preaching is all that devolves upon the Apostle.[35]

God declares the Qur'án to be the revealer of His command and a light of guidance for humanity.

> Thus have we sent the Spirit (Gabriel) to thee with a revelation, by our command. Thou knewest not, ere this, what "the Book" was, or what the faith. But we have ordained it for a light: by it will we guide whom we please of our servants. And thou shalt surely guide into the right way . . .[36]

The Qur'án confirms that Muhammad is revealing the Truth that has caused falsehood to disappear.

> And say: Truth is come and falsehood is vanished. Verily, falsehood is a thing that vanisheth.[37]

To Muhammad's foes who question the authenticity of the Qur'án as a source of divine guidance, the Book itself declares a challenge: Produce a chapter (surah) like it, if you can.

> And if ye be in doubt as to that which we have sent down to our servant, then produce a Sura like it, and summon your witnesses, beside God, if ye are men of truth.[38]

In unequivocal language the Qur'an declares Islam to be the only acceptable path to God.

> Whoso desireth any other religion than Islam, that reli-

gion shall never be accepted from him, and in the next world he shall be among the lost.[39]

The Qur'án declares Islam to be the true religion of God.

The true religion with God is Islam . . .[40]

Islam is announced as the perfect and complete religion.

This day have I perfected your religion for you, and have filled up the measure of my favours upon you: and it is my pleasure that Islam be your religion . . .[41]

Bahá'u'lláh

Bahá'u'lláh announces Himself the Promised One of past religions and the Judge of humankind for this age.

Verily this is that Most Great Beauty, foretold in the Books of the Messengers, through Whom truth shall be distinguished from error and the wisdom of every command shall be tested. Verily He is the Tree of Life that bringeth forth the fruits of God, the Exalted, the Powerful, the Great.[42]

He sees His counsels as the animating force for the advancement of human civilization.

Every man of insight will, in this day, readily admit that the counsels which the Pen of this wronged One hath revealed constitute the supreme animating power for the advancement of the world and the exaltation of its peoples.[43]

Bahá'u'lláh proclaims His Cause as the balance in which the worth and destiny of all are now weighed.

> Say: This is the infallible Balance which the Hand of God is holding, in which all who are in the heavens and all who are on the earth are weighed, and their fate determined, if ye be of them that believe and recognize this truth.[44]

He invites humanity to judge the authenticity of His Revelation by the testimony of past Prophets and Messengers.

> Say: I am come to you, O people, from the Throne of glory, and bear you an announcement from God, the Most Powerful, the Most Exalted, the Most Great. In mine hand I carry the testimony of God, your Lord and the Lord of your sires of old. Weigh it with the just Balance that ye possess, the Balance of the testimony of the Prophets and Messengers of God. If ye find it to be established in truth, if ye believe it to be of God, beware, then, lest ye cavil at it, and render your works vain, and be numbered with the infidels. It is indeed the sign of God that hath been sent down through the power of truth, through which the validity of His Cause hath been demonstrated unto His creatures, and the ensigns of purity lifted up betwixt earth and heaven.[45]

Bahá'u'lláh invites humanity to seek Him now as the light of guidance for this age.

> He that hath Me not is bereft of all things. Turn ye away from all that is on earth and seek none else but Me. I am the Sun of Wisdom and the Ocean of Knowledge. I cheer the faint and revive the dead. I am the guiding Light that illumineth the way.[46]

He observes that recognition of God's Manifestation for each age is the first and foremost duty of each person. Thus, those who do not recognize Him as the Prophet for this age have gone astray – even if they manifest righteous deeds – compared to those who have recognized Him.

> The first duty prescribed by God for His servants is the recognition of Him Who is the Dayspring of His Revelation . . . Whoso achieveth this duty hath attained unto all good; and whoso is deprived thereof hath gone astray, though he be the author of every righteous deed.[47]

Confirming His spiritual unity with other Prophets, Bahá'u'lláh warns that those who reject Him are, in essence, rejecting all the divine educators.

> . . . verily, he who turns away from this Beauty hath also turned away from the Messengers of the past and showeth pride towards God from all eternity to all eternity.[48]

Addressing the kings of the earth, Bahá'u'lláh proclaims His appearance as the sovereign Lord of all and establishes the uniqueness of His Revelation.

> O kings of the earth! He Who is the sovereign Lord of all is come. The Kingdom is God's, the omnipotent Protector, the Self-Subsisting. Worship none but God, and, with radiant hearts, lift up your faces unto your Lord, the Lord of all names. This is a Revelation to which whatever ye possess can never be compared, could ye but know it.[49]

The Light that Shineth in Darkness

The sacred literature of the world is replete with mentions of the concept of light as the vanquisher of darkness and the source of guidance for humanity. At different times God, the divine educators, the holy books and scriptures, or religion itself have all been likened to a light that shines in the darkness of our earthly existence to illuminate the path to salvation and liberation. At times, the focus is on the very source of light – God Himself. More frequently, though, it is the Prophet – the divine educator – who is presented as the beacon of light to humanity. This is probably due to the fact that we can better identify with beings who appear in our likeness as fellow humans and can be physically experienced, than with a transcendent being, a God of whom we can have no conception.

Close examination of the lives of the divine educators reveals that, through their words and deeds, these holy personalities have indeed served as sources of guidance to others. In the process, they have sacrificed their comfort, their material possessions, and at times their very lives to enlighten and save others. By accepting countless sufferings, even tragic deaths, they provide powerful examples of the ideal human being, inspiring their contemporaries and later generations.

Hinduism

Vedic literature declares God (Brahman) to be Light. In Brahman's spiritual kingdom there is no need for luminous objects such as the sun or moon, because the effulgence of the Supreme Lord is there. This effulgence causes continuous illumination of all existence in that kingdom. But in the physical world, the

Lord's spiritual light is covered by material elements; therefore we require the assistance of sun, moon, and artificial light to observe the physical phenomena. In several passages, the Bhagavad Gita confirms this Vedic notion of Brahman as Light: the Spirit Supreme – the transcendent aspect of God or Brahman – acts as the source of light in all luminous objects in our world, including the sun, moon and stars.

> He is the light of all lights which shines beyond all darkness. It is vision, the end of vision, to be reached by vision, dwelling in the heart of all.[1]

> He who remembers the Poet, the Creator, who rules all things from all time, smaller than the smallest atom, but upholding this vast universe, who shines like the sun beyond darkness, far far beyond human thoughts; and at the time of his departure is in union of love and the power of Yoga and, with a mind that wanders not, keeps the power of his life between his eye-brows, he goes to that Spirit Supreme, the Supreme Spirit of Light.[2]

> Supreme Brahman, Light supreme, and supreme purification, Spirit divine eternal, unborn God from the beginning, omnipresent Lord of all.[3]

> If the light of a thousand suns suddenly arose in the sky, that splendour might be compared to the radiance of the Supreme Spirit.[4]

> And even as one sun gives light to all things in this world, so the Lord of the field gives light to all his field.[5]

Other passages in the Bhagavad Gita present Krishna as a source of light.

> By my grace and my wondrous power I have shown to thee Arjuna, this form supreme made of light, which is the Infinite, the All: mine own form from the beginning, never seen by man before.[6]

> That splendour of light that comes from the sun and which illumines the whole universe, the soft light of the moon, the brightness of fire– know that they all come from me.[7]

Buddhism

The role assigned to the Buddha Supreme or Tathagata in Buddhism is comparable to the role of the founder or major Prophet in western religions, or to the Manifestation of God in Bahá'í terminology. The Tathagata is also presented as a light shining in the darkness of this world, providing guidance to a bewildered humanity.

> So long as a Tathagata arises not, an Arahant, a Buddha Supreme, there is no shining forth of great light, of great radiance, but gross darkness of bewilderment prevails, and there is no proclamation of the Four Noble Truths, no teaching, no showing forth, no setting up, no opening up, no analysis, no making plain.
>
> But, brethren, as soon as a Tathagata arises in the world, then there is a shining forth of great light, of great radiance. Then is there no more gloom and darkness of bewilderment; then is there a proclamation of the Four Noble Truths; then is there teaching, a shining forth, a setting up, an opening up, an analysis, a making plain.[8]

Judaism

The author of the Psalms considers God to be his light.

> The LORD is my light and my salvation; whom shall I fear? The LORD is the stronghold of my life; of whom shall I be afraid?[9]

Elsewhere in the same book, God's word is compared to a lamp and a light that guides the author's steps.

> Thy word is a lamp to my feet, and a light to my path.[10]

The author of Proverbs compares God's commandments to a lamp and His teachings to a light.

> For the commandment is a lamp and the teaching a light, and the reproofs of discipline are the way of life.[11]

Isaiah also declares that the Lord will be the everlasting light of Zion (the seat of the Lord's reign, figurative Jerusalem or Israel).

> The sun shall be no more your light by day, nor for brightness shall the moon give light to you by night; but the LORD will be your everlasting light, and your God will be your glory. Your sun shall no more go down, nor your moon withdraw itself; for the LORD will be your everlasting light, and your days of mourning shall be ended.[12]

Christianity

There are a few instances in the New Testament where the Father (God) has been identified as the light.

> Every good endowment and every perfect gift is from above, coming down from the Father of lights with whom there is no variation or shadow due to change.[13]

> This then is the message which we have heard of him, and declare unto you, that God is light, and in him is no darkness at all.[14]

More frequently, though, it is the Son – Jesus – who is presented as the light of this world.

> There was a man sent from God, whose name was John. He came for testimony, to bear witness to the light, that all might believe through him. He was not the light, but came to bear witness to the light. The true light that enlightens every man was coming into the world. He was in the world, and the world was made through him, yet the world knew him not.[15]

> And this is the judgment, that the light [Jesus] has come into the world, and men loved darkness rather than light, because their deeds were evil.[16]

> For it is the God who said, "Let light shine out of darkness," who has shone in our hearts to give the light of the knowledge of the glory of God in the face of Christ.[17]

> And the city has no need of sun or moon to shine upon it, for the glory of God is its light, and its lamp is the Lamb [Jesus].[18]

In other passages, Christ designates Himself as the light of the world.

> As long as I am in the world, I am the light of the world.[19]

> I have come as light into the world, that whoever believes in me may not remain in darkness.[20]

> Again Jesus spoke to them, saying, "I am the light of the world; he who follows me will not walk in darkness, but will have the light of life."[21]

> Jesus said to them, "The light is with you for a little longer. Walk while you have the light, lest the darkness overtake you; he who walks in the darkness does not know where he goes. While you have the light, believe in the light, that you may become sons of light."[22]

Islam

The notion of divine guidance as light is so important in Islam that its Holy Book, the Qur'án, devotes an entire chapter to the subject.[23] *However, Islam shifts the locus of light from the person of the Prophet (as in Christianity) to the Book of God. The Qur'án is repeatedly announced as the Lamp that guides humanity's steps to the Straight Path of God. Allah (God) is, of course, identified as the Source of this Light.*

> God is the LIGHT of the Heavens and of the Earth. His Light is like a niche in which is a lamp – the lamp encased in glass – the glass, as it were, a glistening star. From a blessed tree is it lighted, the olive neither of the East nor of the West, whose oil would well nigh shine out, even though fire touched it not! It is light upon light. God guideth whom He will to His light, and God setteth forth parables to men, for God knoweth all things.[24]

Other passages in the Qur'án appear to point to the revelation itself as the light.

> O men! Now has a proof come to you from your Lord and we have sent down to you a clear light.[25]

> Fain would they put out the light of God with their mouths! But though the Infidels hate it, God will perfect His light.[26]

> . . . and those who shall believe in him [Muhammad] and strengthen him and help him, and follow the light which hath been sent down with him-these are they with whom it shall be well.[27]

> Believe then in God and His Apostle and in the Light which We have sent down; for God is fully aware of all ye do.[28]

Still other verses declare the Qur'án, as the repository of the revelation, to be the light of guidance.

> Thus have we sent the Spirit (Gabriel) to thee with a revelation, by our command. Thou knewest not, ere this, what "the Book" was, or what the faith. But we have ordained it for a light: by it will we guide whom we please of our servants. And thou shalt surely guide into the right way.[29]

> O people of the Scriptures! now is our Apostle come to you to clear up to you much that ye concealed of those Scriptures, and to pass over many things. Now hath a light and a clear Book come to you from God, by which God will guide him who shall follow after his good pleasure, to paths of peace, and will bring them out of the darkness to the light, by his will: and to the straight path will he guide them.[30]

> This Book have we sent down to thee that by their Lord's permission thou mayest bring men out of darkness into light, into the path of the Mighty, the Glorious . . . [31]

On several occasions, the Qur'án also identifies the religion of Moses and His Book as a light and a source of guidance.

> Verily, We have sent down the Law (Towrat*) wherein are guidance and light . . . [32]

> No just estimate do they form of God when they say, "Nothing hath God sent down to man." SAY: Who sent down the Book which Moses brought, a light and guidance to man, which ye set down on paper, publishing part, but concealing most: though ye have now been taught that which neither ye nor your fathers knew? SAY: It is God: then leave them in their pastime of cavillings.[33]

> We gave of old to Moses and Aaron the illumination, and a light and a warning for the God-fearing.[34]

The Bahá'í Faith

The Bahá'í writings also identify God as the heavenly light.

> Thy glory beareth me witness, O Thou, the Light of the world! The fire of Thy love that burneth continually within me hath so inflamed me that whoever among Thy creatures approacheth me, and inclineth his inner ear towards me, cannot fail to hear its raging within each of my veins.[35]

> What I have chosen for myself is what Thou hast Thyself chosen for me, O Thou the Possessor of my soul!" Nay, I find myself to be altogether nothing when face to face with the manifold revelations of Thy names, how much

* Torah.

> less when confronted with the effulgent splendors of the light of Thine own Self.[36]

> O Son of Being! With the hands of power I made thee and with the fingers of strength I created thee; and within thee have I placed the essence of My light. Be thou content with it and seek naught else, for My work is perfect and My commandment is binding. Question it not, nor have a doubt thereof.[37]

> Behold me, then, O my God, how I have fled from myself unto Thee, and have abandoned my own being that I may attain unto the splendors of the light of Thy Being . . . [38]

> . . . within every atom are enshrined the signs that bear eloquent testimony to the revelation of that Most Great Light.[39]

Other passages in the Bahá'í writings present Bahá'u'lláh's revelation as the divine light that guides humanity.

> But God, having stayed their hands, revealed this Light through His sovereign authority and protected it through the power of His might until earth and heaven were illumined by its radiance and brightness.[40]

> Say: "The light hath shone forth from the horizon of Revelation, and the whole earth hath been illumined at the coming of Him Who is the Lord of the Day of the Covenant!" [41]

> O Bethlehem! This Light hath risen in the orient, and traveled towards the occident, until it reached thee in the evening of its life.[42]

> This is the Lamp which the light of Thine own Essence hath lit, and whose radiance the winds of discord can never extinguish.[43]

> Say: In the East the light of His Revelation hath broken; in the West have appeared the signs of His dominion.[44]

> Who is there that can put out the light which the snow-white Hand of God hath lit?[45]

Numerous other passages refer to Bahá'u'lláh Himself as the light of guidance.

> Praise be unto Thee, O my God! Thou seest how He Who is Thy Light hath been shut up in the fortress-town of 'Akká, and been sore oppressed by reason of what the hands of the wicked doers have wrought . . .[46]

> We, in truth, have sent Him Whom We aided with the Holy Spirit that He may announce unto you this Light that hath shone forth from the horizon of the will of your Lord, the Most Exalted, the All-Glorious, and Whose signs have been revealed in the West.[47]

> Verily, this is the Point which God hath ordained to be an ocean of light for the sincere among His servants and a flame of fire to the froward amidst His creatures and the impious among His people . . .[48]

> Indeed He is a Light which is not followed by darkness and a Truth not overtaken by error.[49]

> O Emperor of Austria! He Who is the Dayspring of God's Light dwelt in the prison of 'Akká at the time when thou didst set forth to visit the Aqṣá Mosque (Jerusalem).[50]

Rejection by Humanity

During their ministries, all the divine educators encounter personal hardship, rejection by the masses, active persecution, and even death at the hands of those who oppose them.

Krishna was subjected to persecutions by King Kansa, a tyrant who was determined to destroy Him because he was convinced Krishna would bring about his destruction. Buddha and His early disciples were abused and mocked as they traveled from village to village trying to spread His message. Jesus was called a man possessed by devils and eventually was scourged and crucified. Zoroaster suffered ten years of wandering and struggle before He won His first convert. Muhammad was branded a madman, a deranged poet, and a sorcerer. Bahá'u'lláh was labeled a heretic and a troublemaker. Forced out of His native Persia, He had to endure 40 years of exile, imprisonment, and persecution before He died in a remote land.

Perhaps even more tragic than the physical pain and suffering inflicted on the founders of the great religions are the profound mental anguish and inner agony that these holy figures are forced to endure at the hands of their contemporaries. While the divine educators sacrifice their all for the sake of improving the human condition, an unappreciative humanity deems them mischief-makers, imposters, madmen, magicians, sorcerers, or heretics worthy of persecution, even death. Yet they remain steadfast and true to their mission, despite mankind's ingratitude, and continue to carry out their work with exemplary devotion and self-sacrifice.

Krishna

Krishna laments the fewness of His champions and the smallness of the circle of individuals who have truly known Him.

> Among thousands of men perhaps one strives for perfection; and among thousands of those who strive perhaps one knows me in truth.[1]

Buddha

Buddha's inner anguish yet strong convictions can be felt in the following passage from the Dhammapada.

> I will endure words that hurt in silent peace as the strong elephant endures in battle arrows sent by the bow, for many people lack self-control.[2]

Zoroaster

In the hymn below, Zoroaster first grieves over His rejection by His family and tribe, lamenting His loneliness and the fewness of His allies. Then He asks His only remaining friend, the Wise Lord, for assistance and becomes assured of divine confirmations as the chosen revealer of righteousness in the world.

> To What land shall I flee? Where bend my steps?
> I am thrust out from family and tribe;
> I have no favour from the village to which I would belong,
> Nor from the wicked rulers of the country:
> How then, O Lord, shall I obtain thy favour?
>
> I know, O Wise One, why I am powerless:
> My cattle are few, and I have few men.

> To thee I address my lament: attend unto it, O Lord,
> And grant me the support which friend would give to friend.
> As Righteousness teaches the possession of the Good Mind.
> When, O Wise One, shall the wills of the future saviours come forth,
> The dawns of the days when, through powerful judgment,
> The world shall uphold Righteousness?
> To whom will help come through the Good Mind?
> To me, for I am chosen for the revelation by thee, O Lord.[3]

Moses

Moses not only suffers at the hand of Pharaoh and the Egyptians but is repeatedly rebuked and opposed by His own people. When the Jews see Pharaoh's army chasing and closing in on them near the Red Sea, they cry out in anger at Moses.

> And the people of Israel cried out to the LORD; and they said to Moses, "Is it because there are no graves in Egypt that you have taken us away to die in the wilderness? What have you done to us, in bringing us out of Egypt? Is not this what we said to you in Egypt, 'Let us alone and let us serve the Egyptians'? For it would have been better for us to serve the Egyptians than to die in the wilderness." [4]

About six weeks after their departure from Egypt, the hungry and tired Jews again rebuke Moses and His brother Aaron and express the desire to go back to Egypt.

> And the whole congregation of the people of Israel

murmured against Moses and Aaron in the wilderness, and said to them, "Would that we had died by the hand of the LORD in the land of Egypt, when we sat by the fleshpots and ate bread to the full; for you have brought us out into this wilderness to kill this whole assembly with hunger."[5]

The cry of opposition to Moses is repeated yet again when the Jews reach the Promised Land but are given a false report about its inhabitants by those sent to spy out the land.

Then all the congregation raised a loud cry; and the people wept that night. And all the people of Israel murmured against Moses and Aaron; the whole congregation said to them, "Would that we had died in the land of Egypt! Or would that we had died in this wilderness! Why does the LORD bring us into this land, to fall by the sword? Our wives and our little ones will become a prey; would it not be better for us to go back to Egypt?"[6]

On another occasion two followers refuse to obey a command of Moses and insinuate that, in taking the Jews out of Egypt and promising them a beautiful land, He is motivated by personal ambition.

Is it a small thing that you have brought us out of a land flowing with milk and honey, to kill us in the wilderness, that you must also make yourself a prince over us?[7]

Jesus

During His short ministry Jesus is branded as a heretic by many of His own people and has to be constantly on the move. While this helps Him and His disciples to spread the Word of God, it is physically very taxing.

> And a scribe came up and said to him, "Teacher, I will follow you wherever you go." And Jesus said to him, "Foxes have holes, and birds of the air have nests; but the Son of man has nowhere to lay his head."[8]

Jesus also has to endure repeated insult and degradation.

> For John came neither eating nor drinking, and they say, "He has a demon"; the Son of man came eating and drinking, and they say, "Behold, a glutton and a drunkard, a friend of tax collectors and sinners!" Yet wisdom is justified by her deeds.[9]

While the depth and breadth of Jesus' knowledge and wisdom should be a source of joy and pride to His people, it evidently generates a great deal of resentment among many Jews. Jesus appears resigned to this sad reality.

> And when Jesus had finished these parables, he went away from there, and coming to his own country he taught them in their synagogue, so that they were astonished, and said, "Where did this man get this wisdom and these mighty works? Is not this the carpenter's son? Is not his mother called Mary? And are not his brothers James and Joseph and Simon and Judas? And are not all his sisters with us? Where then did this man get all this?" And they took offense at him. But Jesus said to them, "A prophet is not without honor except in his own country and in his own house."[10]

Some go so far as to call Him possessed and mad.

> Many of them said, "He has a demon, and he is mad; why listen to him?"[11]

Shortly before His crucifixion a depraved foe, unaware of the gravity of its error, puts Jesus through a final series of humiliations and physical abuse. Throughout this cruel treatment, Jesus demonstrates incredible meekness and resignation.

> Again the high priest asked him, "Are you the Christ, the Son of the Blessed?" And Jesus said, "I am; and you will see the Son of man seated at the right hand of Power, and coming with the clouds of heaven. . ." And they all condemned him as deserving death. And some began to spit on him, and to cover his face, and to strike him, saying to him, "Prophesy!" And the guards received him with blows.[12]

> When he had said this, one of the officers standing by struck Jesus with his hand, saying, "Is that how you answer the high priest?" Jesus answered him, "If I have spoken wrongly, bear witness to the wrong; but if I have spoken rightly, why do you strike me?"[13]

> Then they spat on his face, and struck him; and some slapped him . . .[14]

> And the soldiers led him away inside the palace (that is, the praetorium); and they called together the whole battalion. And they clothed him in a purple cloak, and plaiting a crown of thorns they put it on him. And they began to salute him, "Hail, King of the Jews!" And they struck his head with a reed, and spat upon him, and they knelt down in homage to him. And when they had mocked him, they stripped him of the purple cloak, and put his own clothes on him. And they led him out to crucify him.[15]

Muhammad

The Qur'án bears ample testimony to the pattern of rejection and persecution of the divine educators by their own people.

> Oft as an apostle came to them with that for which they had no desire, some they treated as liars, and some they slew . . . [16]

> Because when it was said to them, There is no God but God, they swelled with pride, and said, "Shall we then abandon our gods for a crazed poet?"[17]

> Oh! the misery that rests upon my servants! No apostle cometh to them but they laugh him to scorn.[18]

> . . . each nation schemed against their apostle to lay violent hold on him, and disputed with vain words to refute the truth.[19]

> SAY: Why then have ye of old slain God's prophets, if ye are indeed believers?[20]

Muhammad's claim to reveal verses from God is rejected as a forged calumny, sorcery, something to be shunned.

> For when our distinct signs are recited to them, they say, "This is merely a man who would fain pervert you from your father's Worship." And they say, "This (Koran) is no other than a forged falsehood." And the unbelievers say to the truth when it is presented to them, " 'Tis nothing but palpable sorcery."[21]

> Then said the Apostle, "Oh my Lord! truly my people have esteemed this Koran to be vain babbling." [22]

Like Jesus, Muhammad is also called possessed and mad, yet the Qur'án declares that Muhammad's enemies are the ones who are demented and in manifest error.

> By the PEN and by what they write,
> Thou, O Prophet; by the grace of thy Lord art not possessed!
> And truly a boundless recompense doth await thee,
> For thou art of a noble nature.
> But thou shalt see and they shall see
> Which of you is the demented.
> Now thy Lord! well knoweth He the man who erreth from his path, and well
> doth he know those who have yielded to Guidance . . .[23]

The Qur'án also establishes that there are direct consequences for rejecting Muhammad.

> When thou recitest the Koran we place between thee and those who believe not in the life to come, a dark veil; And we put coverings over their hearts lest they should understand it, and in their ears a heaviness; And when in the Koran thou namest thy One Lord, they turn their backs in flight.[24]

Bahá'u'lláh

Immediately before His exile from Persia at the age of 35, Bahá'u'lláh is arrested and thrown into a dungeon. For four months, His body has to carry the weights of two different chains, one of them weighing about 112 pounds. The marks from these chains stay on His neck for the rest of His life.

> O Shaykh! . . . Shouldst thou at some time happen to visit the dungeon of His Majesty the Sháh, ask the

director and chief jailer to show thee those two chains, one of which is known as Qará-Guhar and the other as Salásil. I swear by the Day-star of Justice that for four months this Wronged One was tormented and chained by one or the other of them. "My grief exceedeth all the woes to which Jacob gave vent, and all the afflictions of Job are but a part of My sorrows!"[25]

All this generation could offer Us were wounds from its darts, and the only cup it proffered to Our lips was the cup of its venom. On our neck We still bear the scar of chains, and upon Our body are imprinted the evidences of an unyielding cruelty.[26]

Bahá'u'lláh is chained to the walls of the dungeon with highwaymen and murderers.

How many the days, O my God, which I have spent in utter loneliness with the transgressors amongst Thy servants, and how many the nights, O my Best-Beloved, during which I lay a captive in the hands of the wayward amidst Thy creatures![27]

Like Jesus and Muhammad, Bahá'u'lláh too is accused of practising magic. He notes that, in bringing such accusations against Him, His contemporaries are making the same mistake as previous generations made and are depriving themselves of God's bounty and grace.

And when We manifest unto you what God hath, through His bountiful favour, bestowed upon Us, ye say, "It is but plain magic." The same words were spoken by the generations that were before you and were what you are, did ye but perceive it. Ye have thereby deprived yourselves of the bounty of God and of His grace, and shall never obtain them till the day when God will have judged between Us and you, and He, verily, is the best of judges.[28]

Bahá'u'lláh testifies that His sufferings have caused even His enemies to grieve.

By the righteousness of God! The tribulations We have sustained are such that any pen that recounteth them cannot but be overwhelmed with anguish. No one of them that truly believe and uphold the unity of God can bear the burden of their recital. So great have been Our sufferings that even the eyes of Our enemies have wept over Us, and beyond them those of every discerning person.[29]

In the passage below, Bahá'u'lláh complains that if His crime is that He has renewed the religion of God, then Moses, Jesus, and Muhammad have committed it before Him.

And if anyone ask them: "For what crime were they imprisoned?" they would answer and say: "They, verily, sought to supplant the Faith with a new religion!" If that which is ancient be what ye prefer, wherefore, then, have ye discarded that which hath been set down in the Torah and the Evangel? Clear it up, O men! By My life! There is no place for you to flee to in this day. If this be My crime, then Muhammad, the Apostle of God, committed it before Me, and before Him He Who was the Spirit of God (Jesus Christ), and yet earlier He Who conversed with God (Moses). And if My sin be this, that I have exalted the Word of God and revealed His Cause, then indeed am I the greatest of sinners! Such a sin I will not barter for the kingdoms of earth and heaven.[30]

Opposition of the Divines

The founders of virtually all the great religions are at odds with the priests of their generation. Many are strongly critical of the religious views and practices of the divines of their age, considering them to be the main hindrance to popular and massive acceptance of the new message. Some go so far as to consider certain of the divines as corrupters of their mother religions.

For instance, witnessing the religious corruption of His time, Zoroaster regards some of the priests (Kavis) and religious leaders (Karapans) of ancient Persia as frustrators of the divine purpose of Ahura Mazda (God). He rebukes them strongly, calling them willfully blind and deaf and accusing them of hindering peace and perfection on earth. The Buddha is also highly critical of certain Brahmins of His time and ridicules their claims to spiritual supremacy. The New Testament describes Jesus' debates with the Jewish doctors from among both the scribes and the Pharisees, whom He calls hypocrites, snakes, and corrupters of the Jewish Faith. Similarly, certain verses in the Qur'án accuse both Jewish and Christian leaders of corruption. In many of His writings, Bahá'u'lláh censures some of the religious leaders of former religions and holds them responsible for the people's rejection of Himself and other divine educators preceding Him.

The history of the major Hebrew traditions (Judaism, Christianity, and Islam) reveals recurring patterns of belief and conduct among the divines that have resulted in each case in the rejection of the claims of the new divine educator. Among them are the following.

Literal interpretation of their sacred texts

The ecclesiastical leaders held preconceived ideas about the future savior promised in their scriptures, ideas often grounded in a literal interpretation of their sacred texts. Thus, when a new claimant such as Jesus of Nazareth failed to fit the preconceived thinking of the Jewish divines, not only did they vehemently oppose Him, but they encouraged the masses of the faithful to do likewise. Similarly, Jewish and Christian religious leaders rejected Muhammad's claims because their literal reading of the Hebrew and Christian scriptures did not allow for an Arab prophet who would usher in a new religious law and who might become a threat to the status and stability of their own traditions. Bahá'u'lláh's claims were also rejected on the same grounds by most Jewish, Christian, and Muslim divines.

Claims of finality

A second factor behind the refusal of most clerics to accept the claim of the new divine educator is the fact that, particularly in Hebrew traditions, ecclesiastical leaders have considered their own religion to be the final religion from God, and their sacred literature as the last authentic revelation. The practical implication of such a world-view is that neither Jews nor Christians nor Muslims expected a new revelation from God. The promises in their scriptures of a future savior or Messiah were to be fulfilled within their own religion. Thus, Jews who did expect a Messiah (many didn't and still do not today), anticipated that He would arise within Judaism. Those Christians who eagerly anticipated the return of Christ expected the Nazarene Jesus to return.

With the advent of Muhammad, both Jewish and Christian leaders refused to accept the message of the Qur'án, as neither group had expected the annullment of their respective laws and a new religious law put in their place. In their view, the laws and teachings of their traditions were sacred and fixed for eternity.

Muslims refuted Jewish and Christian claims to the finality of revelation, but rejected Bahá'u'lláh's claims on the same grounds! Bahá'u'lláh was branded a heretic by Muslim divines, as having the audacity to put forward claims to a post-Muhammadan revelation characterized by numerous innovations, as well as alterations to the Muslim Sharí'a (religious law).

Desire for leadership and fear for their livelihood

In some cases, the priesthood's rejection of the new divine educator has had its roots in their desire for continued leadership of the masses or in having the comfort of a sustained livelihood. Also, many among them must have been conscious of the probable social and economic consequences, for themselves and their families, of allegiance to an unproven message. Either the masses of the faithful would follow the cleric's example and join the new movement, or the cleric would incur the wrath of his co-religionists and be censured and shunned by them. If the latter took place, the risks were high: he would probably experience an immediate loss of power and prestige and be deprived of his source of income. Overnight, he would go from being a respected leader of an established belief system to a hated follower of a new heretical movement. Like the new divine educator, he too would be stripped of his earthly possessions and social standing, and become the object of mockery and persecution. Such considerations must have played a role in the paths chosen by certain religious leaders of the past. Yet, despite the inherent risks and dangers, those few divines who had the foresight to recognize the new divine educator were perhaps conscious of the greater spiritual loss they would experience in this life and in the hereafter should they knowingly reject Him. These individuals have demonstrated tremendous courage in following the example of their newly found leader and accepting the huge challenge of helping others to do likewise.

Zoroaster

Zoroaster complains about the priests of His time who engage in ritual sacrifice and magic. He claims these people are remote from the Good Mind (God) and by their deeds and doctrines are hindering others from attaining peace and perfection.

For these deeds shall ruin overtake
The race of the sacrificers and the magician priests
Through those whom they prevent from living as they would;
These shall be borne far away from them to the dwelling of the Good Mind.[1]

And therefore, the Karapans [religious leaders] are not friendly with the law-abiding. They hinder the cultivation, peace, and perfection of Creation through their own deeds and doctrines.[2]

Buddha

In the following passage, Buddha accuses the Hindu priesthood of misrepresenting Him and His teachings to the Hindu masses.

So saying, bhikkus [Buddhist monks], so proclaiming, I have been baselessly, vainly, falsely, and wrongly misrepresented by some recluses and brahmins thus: "The recluse Gotama is one who leads astray; he teaches the annihilation, the destruction, the extermination of the existent being." As I am not, as I do not proclaim, so have I been baselessly, vainly, falsely, and wrongly misrepresented by some recluses and brahmins . . .[3]

Buddha also points out the Brahmins' preoccupation with religious rites and rituals and their disregard for what lies at the core of religious practice – the purification of one's heart.

Such ways of fastings, couching on the ground,
Bathing at dawn, recitings of the Three (Vedas),
Wearing rough hides, and matted hair and filth,
Chantings and empty rites and penances,
Hypocrisy and cheating and the rod,
Washings, ablutions, rinsings of the mouth, –
These are the caste-marks (vanná) of the brahmin folk,
Things done and practised for some trifling gain.
A heart well tamed, made pure and undefiled,
Considerate for every living thing, –
That is the path to attainment of Brahman.[4]

Jesus

The New Testament contains numerous passages attributed to Jesus in which He shows His displeasure with the Jewish divines, particularly the scribes and Pharisees. In the passages below, Christ claims that the unrighteous divines of His ancestral religion will have no place in His kingdom.

For I tell you, unless your righteousness exceeds that of the scribes and Pharisees, you will never enter the kingdom of heaven.[5]

. . . Jesus said to them, "Truly, I say to you, the tax collectors and the harlots go into the kingdom of God before you. For John came to you in the way of righteousness, and you did not believe him, but the tax collectors and the harlots believed him . . ."[6]

Jesus also strongly condemns the scribes and the Pharisees as workers of iniquity and as hypocrites whose words do not conform to their deeds. He holds them directly responsible for the general aversion of the Jews from His message and from God's kingdom.

> Then said Jesus to the crowds and to his disciples, "The scribes and the Pharisees sit on Moses' seat; so practice and observe whatever they tell you, but not what they do; for they preach, but do not practice. They bind heavy burdens, hard to bear, and lay them on men's shoulders; but they themselves will not move them with their finger. They do all their deeds to be seen by men; for they make their phylacteries broad and their fringes long, and they love the place of honor at feasts and the best seats in the synagogues, and salutations in the market places, and being called rabbi by men."[7]

> But woe to you, scribes and Pharisees, hypocrites! because you shut the kingdom of heaven against men; for you neither enter yourselves, nor allow those who would enter to go in . . . Woe to you, scribes and Pharisees, hypocrites! for you traverse sea and land to make a single proselyte, and when he becomes a proselyte, you make him twice as much a child of hell as yourselves.[8]

Jesus uses a number of colorful analogies. He compares the scribes and Pharisees to whitewashed tombs that are outwardly beautiful but inwardly deadly, and to vipers who suck the blood of the innocent, and to graves upon which men walk unconsciously and fall in.

> Woe to you, scribes and Pharisees, hypocrites! for you are like whitewashed tombs, which outwardly appear beautiful, but within they are full of dead men's bones and all uncleanness. So you also outwardly appear righteous to men, but within you are full of hypocrisy and iniquity.[9]

> Woe to you, scribes and Pharisees, hypocrites! . . . You serpents, you brood of vipers, how are you to escape being sentenced to hell? Therefore I send you prophets and wise men and scribes, some of whom you will kill and crucify, and some you will scourge in your synagogues and persecute from town to town. [10]

> But woe to you Pharisees! for you tithe mint and rue and every herb, and neglect justice and the love of God; these you ought to have done, without neglecting the others. Woe to you Pharisees! for you love the best seat in the synagogues and salutations in the market places. Woe to you! for you are like graves which are not seen, and men walk over them without knowing it.[11]

Needless to say, such severe and unreserved pronouncements against the scribes and Pharisees arouse the hated and enmity of the priests still further. And so when Pontius Pilate offers to release either Jesus or the militant Barabbas, as a gesture of goodwill during the traditional Jewish feast of Passover, they incite the multitude gathered in the Roman barracks to ask for the release of Barabbas.

> Now the chief priests and the elders persuaded the people to ask for Barabbas and destroy Jesus. The governor again said to them, "Which of the two do you want me to release for you?" And they said, "Barabbas." Pilate said to them, "Then what shall I do with Jesus who is called Christ?" They all said, "Let him be crucified." And he said, "Why, what evil has he done?" But they shouted all the more, "Let him be crucified." So when Pilate saw that he was gaining nothing, but rather that a riot was beginning, he took water and washed his hands before the crowd, saying, "I am innocent of this man's blood . . ."[12]

Muhammad

The Qur'án corroborates Jesus' view of the Jewish priests and elders and, in turn, attributes the same kind of misbehavior to Christian divines. Both groups are condemned as perpetrators of evil and iniquity and as individuals who have led their people astray.

> O Believers! of a truth, many of the teachers and monks do devour man's substance in vanity, and turn them from the Way of God. But to those who treasure up gold and silver and expend it not in the Way of God, announce tidings of a grievous torment. On that day their treasures shall be heated in hell fire, and their foreheads, and their sides, and their backs, shall be branded with them. . . . "This is what ye have treasured up for yourselves: taste, therefore, your treasures!"[13]

> And they shall say: "Oh our Lord! indeed we obeyed our chiefs and our great ones, and they misled us from the way of God – O our Lord! give them a double chastisement, and curse them with a heavy curse."[14]

> "The hand of God," say the Jews, "is chained up." Chained up be their own hands! And for that which they have said, they were accursed. Nay, outstretched are both His hands!"[15]

Bahá'u'lláh

Bahá'u'lláh too was opposed by the divines of His mother religion, Islam. He felt that the divines of previous religious traditions acted as a veil between Him and their people.

> Turn unto God and seek His protection, O concourse of

divines, and make not of yourselves a veil between Me and My creatures.[16]

Bahá'u'lláh also declares that, in each age, the divines have played an active role in persecuting the new messengers:

Consider the former generations. Witness how every time the Day Star of Divine bounty hath shed the light of His Revelation upon the world, the people of His Day have arisen against Him, and repudiated His truth. They who were regarded as the leaders of men have invariably striven to hinder their followers from turning unto Him Who is the Ocean of God's limitless bounty.

Behold how the people, as a result of the verdict pronounced by the divines of His age, have cast Abraham, the Friend of God, into fire; how Moses, He Who held converse with the Almighty, was denounced as liar and slanderer. Reflect how Jesus, the Spirit of God, was, notwithstanding His extreme meekness and perfect tender-heartedness, treated by His enemies. So fierce was the opposition which He, the Essence of Being and Lord of the visible and invisible, had to face, that He had nowhere to lay His head. He wandered continually from place to place, deprived of a permanent abode.

Ponder that which befell Muhammad, the Seal of the Prophets, may the life of all else be a sacrifice unto Him. How severe the afflictions which the leaders of the Jewish people and of the idol-worshipers caused to rain upon Him, Who is the sovereign Lord of all, in consequence of His proclamation of the unity of God and of the truth of His Message![17]

Bahá'u'lláh states that religious leaders often lead themselves and others astray by either clinging to the literal meaning of certain scriptural verses whose inner meanings they do not understand, or by their lust for leadership or worldly possessions:

> . . . know of a certainty that the people in every age, clinging to a verse of the Book, have uttered such vain and absurd sayings, contending that no Prophet should again be made manifest to the world. Even as the Christian divines . . . have sought to explain that the law of the Gospel shall at no time be annulled, and that no independent Prophet shall again be made manifest, unless He confirmeth the law of the Gospel . . . the people of the Qur'án, like unto the people of old, have allowed the words "Seal of the Prophets" to veil their eyes. And yet, they themselves testify to this verse: "None knoweth the interpretation thereof but God and they that are well-grounded in knowledge." [Qur'an 3:5-7]. . . Such deeds and words have been solely instigated by leaders of religion, they that worship no God but their own desire, who bear allegiance to naught but gold, who are wrapt in the densest veils of learning, and who, enmeshed by its obscurities, are lost in the wilds of error.[18]

> Leaders of religion, in every age, have hindered their people from attaining the shores of eternal salvation, inasmuch as they held the reins of authority in their mighty grasp. Some for the lust of leadership, others through want of knowledge and understanding, have been the cause of the deprivation of the people. By their sanction and authority, every Prophet of God hath drunk from the chalice of sacrifice . . .[19]

Sacrificial Lambs

Suffering and sacrifice have been the lot of all the founders of the great religions. Without exception, they give up personal freedom and comfort. Some leave behind family and friends, others abandon lives of luxury and material riches, and still others sacrifice their very lives for the cause they promote. Remarkably, their primary purpose in making these sacrifices is humanity's redemption from itself by slowly transforming its character and helping human beings to manifest their true identity – that of primarily spiritual beings experiencing a temporary physical life on this planet in an eternal journey toward the ultimate reality. By providing a living example of detachment and sacrifice, these holy figures have helped us human beings gradually reveal the virtues with which our souls are invested.

Buddha

Having sacrificed so much material well-being so that others may live a better life, Buddha reveals His acceptance of suffering.

> I will endure words that hurt in silent peace as the strong elephant endures in battle arrows sent by the bow, for many people lack self-control.[1]

Zoroaster

Zoroaster foretells His sufferings at the hands of His opponents in the early days of His ministry.

> As the holy one I recognized thee, O Wise Lord,
> When he came to me as Good Mind,
> When first I was instructed in your word.
> Suffering among men will be caused to me by my zeal
> To carry out that which you tell me is the greatest good.[2]

Moses

Moses recounts His sufferings at the hands of His followers, whose sin of forgetting God and returning to idol worship in Moses' absence forces Him to go back to Mount Sinai and endure another forty days and nights of anguish and deprivation before God reveals the Ten Commandments to Him a second time.

> So, I turned and came down from the mountain, and the mountain was burning with fire; and the two tables of the covenant were in my two hands. And I looked, and behold, you had sinned against the LORD your God; you had made yourselves a molten calf; you had turned aside quickly from the way which the LORD had commanded you. So I took hold of the two tables, and cast them out of my two hands, and broke them before your eyes. Then I lay prostrate before the LORD as before, forty days and forty nights; I neither ate bread nor drank water, because of all the sin which you had committed, in doing what was evil in the sight of the LORD . . . because the LORD had said he would destroy you. And I prayed to the LORD, "O Lord GOD, destroy not thy people and thy heritage, whom thou hast redeemed through thy greatness, whom thou hast brought out of Egypt with a mighty hand."[3]

Time and again, throughout His 40-year ordeal, Moses bears the wrath of God on behalf of His ungrateful followers. God repeatedly sacrifices Moses to teach His erring followers important spiritual lessons.

> But the LORD was angry with me on your account, and would not hearken to me; and the LORD said to me, "Let it suffice you; speak no more to me of this matter. Go up to the top of Pisgah,* and lift up your eyes westward and northward and southward and eastward, and behold it with your eyes; for you shall not go over this Jordan."[4]

> Furthermore the LORD was angry with me on your account, and he swore that I should not cross the Jordan, and that I should not enter the good land which the LORD your God gives you for an inheritance. For I must die in this land, I must not go over the Jordan; but you shall go over and take possession of that good land.[5]

Jesus

Even while breathing His last on the cross, Christ is still aware of His mission and is discharging His spiritual obligation of trying to save a depraved humanity from the burden of its sins – sins that have perhaps reached their height with the cruel punishment and crucifixion of its Savior.

> Then said Jesus, "Father, forgive them; for they know not what they do."[6]

The New Testament indicates that Jesus was fully aware of His destiny.

> ". . . for this is my blood of the covenant, which is poured out for many for the forgiveness of sins . . ."[7]

---

* The mountain where Moses sees the Promised Land for the first time.

The Apostle Paul confirms Christ's important role in history as a sacrifice for human sins.

> But God shows his love for us in that while we were yet sinners Christ died for us.[8]

Years earlier, John the Baptist had foreseen his cousin's destiny while seeing Him walk by.

> Behold, the Lamb of God, who takes away the sin of the world![9]

Jesus Himself testifies to His role as a sacrifice for humanity.

> I am the good shepherd. The good shepherd lays down his life for the sheep. He who is a hireling and not a shepherd, whose own the sheep are not, sees the wolf coming and leaves the sheep and flees; and the wolf snatches them and scatters them. He flees because he is a hireling and cares nothing for the sheep.[10]

Muhammad

Distressed by rejection and the lies His people have directed at him, Muhammad turns to God for assistance. God reminds him that previous Prophets have been through the same kinds of ordeal and invites Muhammad to be patient until divine assistance comes.

> . . . But it is not merely thee whom they charge with falsehood, but the ungodly gainsay the signs of God. Before thee have apostles already been charged with falsehood: but they bore the charge and the wrong with constancy, till our help came to them . . .[11]

Bahá'u'lláh dwells on the sufferings of Muhammad.

> For this reason did Muhammad cry out: "No Prophet of God hath suffered such harm as I have suffered." And in the Qur'án are recorded all the calumnies and reproaches uttered against Him, as well as all the afflictions which He suffered . . . In the midst of His agony, the Voice of Gabriel . . . was heard saying: "But if their opposition be grievous to Thee – if thou canst, seek out an opening into the earth or a ladder into heaven" (Qur'án 6:35). The implication of this utterance is that His case had no remedy, that they would not withhold their hands from Him unless he should hide Himself beneath the depths of the earth, or take His flight unto heaven.[12]

Bahá'u'lláh

Bahá'u'lláh recounts the tales of His own sufferings and imprisonment at the hands of His enemies.

> Ponder a while on the woes and afflictions which this Prisoner hath sustained. I have, all the days of My life, been at the mercy of Mine enemies, and have suffered each day, in the path of the love of God, a fresh tribulation.[13]

Bahá'u'lláh announces that He has accepted a cruel destiny to help transform His fellow human beings and free them from the bondage of self so that they can achieve true liberty.

> We have accepted to be tried by ills and troubles, that ye may sanctify yourselves from all earthly defilements. Why, then, refuse ye to ponder Our purpose in your hearts? By the righteousness of God! Whoso will reflect upon the tribulations We have suffered, his soul will assuredly melt away with sorrow. Thy Lord Himself beareth witness to the truth of My words. We have sus-

> tained the weight of all calamities to sanctify you from all earthly corruption, and ye are yet indifferent.[14]

> My body hath endured imprisonment that ye may be released from the bondage of self.[15]

> The Ancient Beauty hath consented to be bound with chains that mankind may be released from its bondage, and hath accepted to be made a prisoner within this most mighty Stronghold that the whole world may attain unto true liberty. He hath drained to its dregs the cup of sorrow, that all the peoples of the earth may attain unto abiding joy, and be filled with gladness.[16]

Like Christ and other divine educators, Bahá'u'lláh confirms His salvific role.

> We, verily, have come for your sakes, and have borne the misfortunes of the world for your salvation.[17]

He has come to build a new, global civilization but His enemies have cast Him into exile and imprisonment.

> We have accepted to be abased, O believers in the Unity of God, that ye may be exalted, and have suffered manifold afflictions, that ye might prosper and flourish. He Who hath come to build anew the whole world, behold, how they that have joined partners with God have forced Him to dwell within the most desolate of cities![18]

Continuity with the Past

The great religions of the world are not born in a vacuum. The continuity of human history dictates the existence of a parent religion for each of the great traditions. Hinduism and Zoroastrianism came out of the matrix of the Vedic religions of the Aryan people. Hinduism, in turn, became the parent religion of Buddhism. The religion of Moses had a direct link to those of His Hebrew predecessors such as Abraham and Noah. The founder of Christianity was first a Jew. Islam was born in the Middle East with its Judeo-Christian traditions and Zoroastrian influences. The Bahá'í Faith was revealed in the heart of Islam.

Thus it is not remarkable that the message of each religious dispensation is presented in a language and context already familiar to its contemporaries. This often means strong linguistic, doctrinal, and ideological ties between the mother religion and the new revelation. Hence, in expressing His world-view, the Buddha makes use of Hindu terms, concepts, and myths. Yet, at the same time, Buddha's teachings cause the emergence of a new and, in time, independent system of belief.

Additionally, through the ages, the territorial expansionism of great military powers such as the Persians, the Arabs, the Mongols and the Turks, and their occupation of lands in the Far East including India, have often resulted in the cross-fertilization of eastern and western religions and ideological exchanges that have created ties and reinforced already existing parallels between them. All of these have resulted in common threads among eastern and western religions and also ensured continuity throughout religious history.

Hinduism

Krishna explains the link between His revelation and those of His predecessors.

> I revealed this everlasting Yoga to Vivasvan, the sun, the father of light. He in turn revealed it to Manu, his son, the father of man. And Manu taught his son, king Ikshvaku, the saint. Then it was taught from father to son in the line of kings who were saints; but in the revolutions of times immemorial this doctrine was forgotten by men. Today I am revealing to thee this Yoga eternal, this secret supreme: because of thy love for me, and because I am thy friend.[1]

Buddhism

Buddha identifies His Noble Eightfold Path with the ancient path of past Enlightened Ones who have preceded Him.

> Even so, brethren, have I seen an ancient Path, an ancient track traversed by the Perfectly Enlightened Ones of the past. And what, brethren, is that ancient Path? It is the Noble Eightfold Path.[2]

Judaism

God affirms the continuity of the Hebrew tradition to the Israelites by asking Moses to inform His people that He is the same God whom their forefathers worshipped.

> God also said to Moses, "Say this to the people of Israel, 'The LORD, the God of your fathers, the God of Abraham, the God of Isaac, and the God of Jacob, has sent me to you . . .' "[3]

Christianity

Jesus establishes a direct link between His revelation and that of Moses. He also corroborates that His words and teachings are in harmony with the writings of Moses.

> If you believed Moses, you would believe me, for he wrote of me. But if you do not believe his writings, how will you believe my words?[4]

Jesus proclaims His continuity with the past by announcing His role as the fulfiller, not abrogator, of the Mosaic Law.

> Think not that I have come to abolish the law and the prophets; I have come not to abolish them but to fulfil them. For truly, I say to you, till heaven and earth pass away, not an iota, not a dot, will pass from the law until all is accomplished.[5]

The Apostle Paul ties the appearance of the Son to those of the ancient Hebrew prophets.

> In many and various ways God spoke of old to our fathers by the prophets; but in these last days he has spoken to us by a Son, whom he appointed the heir of all things, through whom also he created the world.[6]

Islam

Several passages in the Qur'án identify Islam with the primordial religion of God brought to humanity by other Prophets who preceded Muhammad. The Qur'án makes it clear that Muhammad's Path, the true (3: 17) and perfect (5: 5) religion of God, is the same Path as that of the Hebrew prophets before Him (42: 11).

All the major Hebrew prophets or their followers have been called Muslims in the Qur'án. This includes Noah (10: 73), Abraham (2: 126) Moses and His followers (10: 84, 10: 90, 7: 123), and the Disciples of Christ (5: 111).

> Nothing hath been said to thee which hath not been said of old to apostles before thee.[7]

> Verily we have revealed to thee as we revealed to Noah and the Prophets after him, and as we revealed to Abraham, and Ismaël, and Isaac, and Jacob, and the tribes, and Jesus, and Job, and Jonah, and Aaron, and Solomon; and to David gave we Psalms.[8]

> Already have apostles before me come to you with miracles, and with that of which ye speak. Wherefore slew ye them? Tell me, if ye are men of truth.[9]

> To you hath He prescribed the faith which He commanded unto Noah, and which we have revealed to thee, and which we commanded unto Abraham and Moses and Jesus, saying, "Observe this faith, and be not divided into sects therein." Intolerable to those who worship idols jointly with God.[10]

The Bahá'í Faith

Bahá'u'lláh's religious world-view admits an unbroken link between all the divinely ordained religions of the past, present, and future. He sees the great religions of the world as different manifestations of the one and only religion ever revealed by God. Connecting His own dispensation to those of the past and the future, He proclaims:

> This is the changeless Faith of God, eternal in the past, eternal in the future.[11]

He also anticipates an uninterruptable chain of successive revelations in the future that will ensure the continuous flow of God's grace to humanity.

> These Mirrors [the divine educators] will everlastingly succeed each other, and will continue to reflect the light of the Ancient of Days . . . for the Grace of God can never cease from flowing. This is a truth that none can disprove.[12]

With the above proclamation, Bahá'u'lláh leaves no room for His followers to fall into the "last revelation" trap that has plagued the adherents of past traditions. Bahá'ís do not claim finality either for Bahá'u'lláh or for His revelation.

Bahá'u'lláh confirms the oneness and spiritual unity of all the Prophets, regardless of their specific faiths or where they appeared. This teaching can potentially strengthen the already existing ties among the eastern and western religions.

> The Bearers of the Trust of God are made manifest unto the peoples of the earth as the Exponents of a new Cause and the Revealers of a new Message. Inasmuch as these Birds of the celestial Throne are all sent down from the heaven of the Will of God, and as they all arise to proclaim His irresistible Faith, they, therefore, are regarded as one soul and the same person. For they all drink from the one Cup of the love of God, and all partake of the fruit of the same Tree of Oneness.[13]

> Know thou assuredly that the essence of all the Prophets of God is one and the same. Their unity is absolute. God, the Creator, saith: There is no distinction whatsoever

among the Bearers of My Message. They all have but one purpose; their secret is the same secret. To prefer one in honor to another, to exalt certain ones above the rest, is in no wise to be permitted. Every true Prophet hath regarded His Message as fundamentally the same as the Revelation of every other Prophet gone before Him.[14]

Future Saviors

The sacred literature of most religions foresees the advent of other holy figures who are to appear in distant futures to continue to provide humanity with spiritual guidance through the ages. There are also references to the appearance of a universal manifestation at the end of time who will gather all the nations together and establish a global, paradisal community on earth characterized by peace, justice, and enlightenment.

With regard to the coming of future divine educators, Krishna speaks of His own cyclical reappearance in the form of future avatars (returns) to destroy evil. Zoroastrian scriptures promise the advent of the Saoshyant (One who will bring benefit) who will renew the world. Buddhist sutras speak of the coming of future Buddhas, particularly the Maitreya or Metteyya (He whose name is kindness). Many Jews anticipate the advent of the Lord of Hosts (Rabb-al-Junúd) who will gather and judge all the nations. Christ foretold His own return or the coming of the Son of man, whom He also called the Spirit of Truth and the Counselor or Comforter. The Qur'án sets a limit on the duration of all religious dispensations and anticipates future messengers. Muslim traditions speak of the advent of Imam Mahdi (the Rightly Guided One) who will be of Muhammad's own lineage and will establish a new religion. Bahá'u'lláh states that there will be no end to the appearance of future manifestations.

Hinduism

Krishna anticipates His cyclical returns for the establishment of righteousness in the world.

> When righteousness is weak and faints and unrighteousness exults in pride, then my Spirit arises on earth. For the salvation of those who are good, for the destruction of evil in men, for the fulfillment of the kingdom of righteousness, I come to this world in the ages that pass.[1]

Zoroastrianism

The followers of Zoroaster are promised the appearance of a future Prophet, a universal manifestation for the whole of humanity. He will regenerate the human race and the entire physical world will benefit from His appearance.

> He shall be the victorious Benefactor (Saoshyant) by name and World-renovator (Astavat-ereta) by name. He is Benefactor because he will benefit the entire physical world; he is World-renovator because he will establish the physical living existence indestructible. He will oppose the evil of the progeny of the biped and withstand the enmity produced by the faithful.[2]

Buddhism

Buddha also refers to the appearance of a future Buddha, the Metteyya Buddha who will be accompanied by thousands of monks (not hundreds, as with His own appearance).

> And in that time . . . there will arise in the world a Blessed Lord, an Arahant fully-enlightened Buddha named Metteyya, endowed with wisdom and conduct, a Well-Farer, Knower of the worlds, incomparable Trainer of men to be tamed, Teacher of gods and humans, enlightened and blessed, just as I am now. He will thoroughly know by his own super-knowledge, and proclaim, this

> universe with its devas and maras and Brahmas, its ascetics and Brahmins, and this generation with its princes and people, just as I do now. He will teach the Dhamma, lovely in its beginning, lovely in its middle, lovely in its ending, in the spirit and in the letter, and proclaim, just as I do now, the holy life in its fullness and purity. He will be attended by a company of thousands of monks, just as I am attended by a company of hundreds.[3]

> And Ananda . . . said to the Blessed One: "Who shall teach us when thou art gone?" And the Blessed One replied: "I am not the first Buddha who came upon the earth, nor shall I be the last. In due time another Buddha will arise in the world, a Holy One, a supremely enlightened One, endowed with wisdom in conduct, auspicious, knowing the universe, an incomparable leader of men, a master of angels and mortals. He will reveal to you the same eternal truths which I have taught you. He will preach his religion, glorious in its origin, glorious at the climax, and glorious at the goal, in the spirit and in the letter. He will proclaim a religious life, wholly perfect and pure; such as I now proclaim." Ananda said: "How shall we know him?" The Blessed One said: "He will be known as Metteyya, which means 'he whose name is kindness.'"[4]

Judaism

Moses promises His people that, in due time, another Prophet like him will be raised by God.

> The Lord your God will raise up for you a prophet like me from among you, from your brethren – him you shall heed . . .[5]

God confirms to Moses that He has spoken well.

> And Jehovah said unto me, They have well said that which they have spoken. I will raise them up a prophet from among their brethren, like unto thee; and I will put my words in his mouth, and he shall speak unto them all that I shall command him. And it shall come to pass, that whosoever will not hearken unto my words which he shall speak in my name, I will require it of him.[6]

The Hebrew prophet Daniel describes his vision of a future Prophet who will establish a global kingdom on earth, encompassing the people of all nations and languages.

> I saw in the night visions, and behold, with the clouds of heaven there came one like a son of man, and he came to the Ancient of Days and was presented before him. And to him was given dominion and glory and kingdom, that all peoples, nations, and languages should serve him; his dominion is an everlasting dominion, which shall not pass away, and his kingdom one that shall not be destroyed.[7]

Another Hebrew prophet, Isaiah, has similar visions of a future Prophet who will establish a lasting kingdom on earth characterized by peace, justice, and righteousness.

> For to us a child is born, to us a son is given; and the government will be upon his shoulder, and his name will be called "Wonderful Counselor, Mighty God, Everlasting Father, Prince of Peace." Of the increase of his government and of peace there will be no end, upon the throne of David, and over his kingdom, to establish it, and to uphold it with justice and with righteousness from this time forth and for evermore. The zeal of the LORD of hosts will do this.[8]

According to Isaiah, this Prophet will act as the judge of all nations. During His era war will cease between nations and former foes will turn into friends:

> He shall judge between the nations, and shall decide for many peoples; and they shall beat their swords into plowshares, and their spears into pruning hooks; nation shall not lift up sword against nation, neither shall they learn war any more.[9]

> The wolf also shall dwell with the lamb, and the leopard shall lie down with the kid; and the calf and the young lion and the fatling together; and a little child shall lead them.[10]

God Himself promises to gather all the nations and languages together in the future.

> For I know their works and their thoughts, and I am coming to gather all nations and tongues; and they shall come and shall see my glory.[11]

Christianity

Jesus foretells the appearance of a future divine educator who will glorify Him and guide the nations. He calls this personage by different titles including the Spirit of Truth, the Son of man, the Counselor, the Comforter, and the Holy Spirit.

> I have yet many things to say to you, but you cannot bear them now. When the Spirit of truth comes, he will guide you into all the truth; for he will not speak on his own authority, but whatever he hears he will speak, and he will declare to you the things that are to come. He will glorify me, for he will take what is mine and declare

> it to you. All that the Father has is mine; therefore I said that he will take what is mine and declare it to you.[12]

Christ warns His followers to be constantly watching for the appearance of this future educator, for He will come when least expected. Affirming the essential unity of the Prophets, Jesus uses the same honorary title for this future educator that He preferred for Himself – namely, the Son of man.[13]

> As were the days of Noah, so will be the coming of the Son of man. For as in those days before the flood they were eating and drinking, marrying and giving in marriage, until the day when Noah entered the ark, and they did not know until the flood came and swept them all away, so will be the coming of the Son of man . . . Watch therefore, for you do not know on what day your Lord is coming. But know this, that if the householder had known in what part of the night the thief was coming, he would have watched and would not have let his house be broken into. Therefore you also must be ready; for the Son of man is coming at an hour you do not expect.[14]

> Watch therefore, for you know neither the day nor the hour.[15]

Christ confesses that even He has no knowledge of when the future educator will appear. Only God, the Father, knows.

> But of that day or that hour no one knows, not even the angels in heaven, nor the Son, but only the Father.[16]

Jesus does however give His disciples details of the apocalyptic events that are to precede the appearance of the Son of man.

> For then shall be great tribulation, such as was not since the beginning of the world to this time, no, nor ever shall be . . . But immediately after the tribulation of those days the sun shall be darkened, and the moon shall not give her light, and the stars shall fall from heaven, and the powers of the heavens shall be shaken: and then shall appear the sign of the Son of man in heaven: and then shall all the tribes of the earth mourn, and they shall see the Son of man coming on the clouds of heaven with power and great glory. And he shall send forth his angels with a great sound of a trumpet, and they shall gather together his elect from the four winds, from one end of heaven to the other.[17]

More details of the circumstances surrounding the apocalyptic appearance of the Son of man is given by the author of the Book of Revelation.

> And I saw a new heaven and a new earth: for the first heaven and the first earth are passed away; and the sea is no more. And I saw the holy city, new Jerusalem, coming down out of heaven of God, made ready as a bride adorned for her husband . . . And he carried me away in the Spirit to a mountain great and high, and showed me the holy city Jerusalem, coming down out of heaven from God . . . And the city hath no need of the sun, neither of the moon, to shine upon it: for the glory of God did lighten it, and the lamp thereof *is* the Lamb. And the nations shall walk amidst the light thereof: and the kings of the earth bring their glory into it. And the gates thereof shall in no wise be shut by day (for there shall be no night there).[18]

Islam

The Qur'án anticipates the appearance of other Prophets after Muhammad.

> O children of Adam! There shall come to you apostles from among yourselves, rehearsing My signs to you; and whoso shall fear God and do good works, no fear shall be upon them, neither shall they be put to grief.[19]

> . . . if Guidance shall come to you from me, whoso shall follow my guidance, on them shall come no fear, neither shall they be grieved: But they who shall not believe, and treat our signs as false-hoods, these shall be inmates of the fire; in it shall they remain for ever.[20]

The Qur'án notes that all peoples[21] *have had their own divine educators.*

> And every people hath had its apostle. And when their apostle came, a rightful decision took place between them, and they were not wronged.[22]

> Verily we have sent thee with the truth; a bearer of good tidings and a warner; nor hath there been a people unvisited by its warner.[23]

The Qur'án also declares that every nation (religious dispensation) has a finite duration that cannot be lengthened or shortened.

> Every nation hath its set time. And when their time is come, they shall not retard it an hour; and they shall not advance it.[24]

> Neither too soon, nor too late, shall a people reach its appointed time.[25]

Also, in the Qur'án God declares that He has set Islam as not the last religion, but one in the middle or center of religious dispensations, implying that as many nations (religions) as preceded Islam will appear after it.

> Thus have we made you a central people, that ye may be witnesses in regard to mankind, and that the apostle may be a witness in regard to you.[26]

The Bahá'í Faith

Bahá'u'lláh emphasizes that divine educators have always appeared among humankind and this will not change in the future. He considers the appearance of these sources of guidance as the greatest outpouring of divine grace and mercy.

> Can one of sane mind ever seriously imagine that, in view of certain words the meaning of which he cannot comprehend, the portal of God's infinite guidance can ever be closed in the face of men? Can he ever conceive for these Divine Luminaries, these resplendent Lights either a beginning or an end? What outpouring flood can compare with the stream of His all-embracing grace, and what blessing can excel the evidences of so great and pervasive a mercy?[27]

He prophesies the appearance of divine educators to come after Him, but no sooner than a full millennium from His own advent.

> Whoso layeth claim to a Revelation direct from God, ere the expiration of a full thousand years, such a man is assuredly a lying imposter.[28]

Bahá'u'lláh considers His own advent to be the fulfillment of the prophecies of all past scriptures which foretell the coming of a Holy One who will gather together all the nations.

The Revelation which, from time immemorial, hath been acclaimed as the Purpose and Promise of all the Prophets of God, and the most cherished Desire of His Messengers, hath now, by virtue of the pervasive Will of the Almighty and at His irresistible bidding, been revealed unto men. The advent of such a Revelation hath been heralded in all the sacred Scriptures. Behold how, notwithstanding such an announcement, mankind hath strayed from its path and shut out itself from its glory.[29]

Render thanks unto God, inasmuch as ye have attained unto your heart's Desire, and been united to Him Who is the Promise of all nations.[30]

Behold, how the divers peoples and kindreds of the earth have been waiting for the coming of the Promised One. No sooner had He, Who is the Sun of Truth, been made manifest, than, lo, all turned away from Him, except them whom God was pleased to guide.[31]

Verily I say, this is the Day in which mankind can behold the Face, and hear the Voice, of the Promised One.[32]

Great indeed is this Day! The allusions made to it in all the sacred Scriptures as the Day of God attest its greatness. The soul of every Prophet of God, of every Divine Messenger, hath thirsted for this wondrous Day. All the divers kindreds of the earth have, likewise, yearned to attain it.[33]

Carmel hath, in this Day, hastened in longing adoration to attain His court, whilst from the heart of Zion there cometh the cry: "The promise is fulfilled. That which had been announced in the holy Writ of God, the most Exalted, the Almighty, the Best-Beloved, is made manifest."[34]

By Him Who is the Great Announcement! The All-Merciful is come invested with undoubted sovereignty. The Balance hath been appointed, and all them that dwell on earth have been gathered together. The Trumpet hath been blown, and lo, all eyes have stared up with terror, and the hearts of all who are in the heavens and on the earth have trembled, except them whom the breath of the verses of God hath quickened, and who have detached themselves from all things.[35]

Brief Lives of the Divine Educators

Many readers will be unfamiliar with the lives and teachings of some of the central figures of the world religions. The following accounts provide brief sketches only; moreover, neither believers nor modern scholars agree on all details. Despite this, we have felt it better to provide some contextual framework; readers who wish to learn more about the major world religions and their founders are referred to the books listed in the Bibliography.

Krishna (KRSNA)

Krishna (Sanskrit name: "black" or "dark") can best be described as a composite figure in the history and sacred literature of Hinduism. He is not the founder of Hinduism: the Hindu religious tradition is much more ancient than Krishna and is the only world religion with no established founder.

Today, as the most celebrated incarnation of Vishnu (see below), Krishna is perhaps the most widely worshipped figure in all India. A wide-ranging body of art, literature, and devotional practices has been developed around His person. Yet Krishna can be properly understood only through an understanding of Hindu theology and the interplay between the Hindu deities, humanity, and the world of existence.

The position and role of Krishna in Hindu theology and cosmology

The earliest known mention of Krishna is in the Rig Veda

(1500–1200 B.C.E.), but He is not a prominent figure there and not presented as divine. The four Vedas are the most ancient Hindu scriptures (ranging from 1500–400 B.C.E.). They identify a pantheon of gods, but Krishna is not among them. Major Vedic deities include:

- Indra: god of rain, thunder, and war; the most frequently invoked Vedic god
- Agni: god of fire and sacrifice
- Varuna (later becomes Brahma): creator and preserver of the cosmos
- Mitra: the sun god (corresponding to the Iranian god Mithra)
- Vishnu: known for his ability to appear in the physical world in various human incarnations (avatars); later Krishna becomes the most famous of these incarnations
- Rudra (later becomes Shiva): has two opposite aspects, one destructive, the other healing.

Most contemporary Hindu scholars agree that all these Vedic gods should be viewed as different aspects or powers of Brahman – the Supreme Vedic Deity. The Rig Veda itself appears to confirm this:

> He [Brahman] is one, though wise men call Him by many names.[1]

The Hindu desire to make the transcendent figure of Brahman more accessible to human understanding led to His gradual transformation in religious thought. Over time, the remote, impersonal Brahman of the Vedas gives way to a personal and more immanent God known as Ishvara (Lord) who is present in the world, participates in human affairs and, when needed, intervenes to restore balance in the cosmos. Ishvara even takes on human characteristics through a triad of divine figures who accept earthly lives and go so far as to form families. The Ishvara triad (Trimurti) of deities consisted of:

- Brahma: Varuna of the Vedas, the creator of the universe
- Vishnu: the preserver of the cosmos
- Shiva: the destroyer and yet also the re-creator of the world

The rise of Ishvara and subsequent decline of Brahman's pre-eminence in Hindu thought signaled the gradual prominence of non-Aryan gods in Hinduism. The three-fold activities of Ishvara, bringing rhythm to the world through Brahma, Vishnu, and Shiva, are critical to an understanding of the Hindu belief in the need for the cyclical creation and destruction of the world.

The driving forces behind the shift from the ineffable Brahman to the immanent Ishvara were the epic poems *Mahabharata* (literally "Great King Bharata"), and Hindu folk tales known as the *Puranas* ("that which gives accounts of the past"). However, soon the Zoroastrian notion of *avatars* also found its way into the Hindu texts. In particular, the followers of Vishnu began to believe in the cyclical reappearance of their Lord on earth in the physical form of human figures who appear at the end of each Hindu cycle when evil has overtaken the world. Their advent signals the destruction of the old cycle, the restoration of cosmic order, and the beginning of a new era of righteousness. Krishna confirms this in the Bhagavad Gita:

> When righteousness is weak and faints and unrighteousness exults in pride, then my Spirit arises on Earth. For the salvation of those who are good, for the destruction of evil in men, for the fulfilment of the kingdom of righteousness, I come to this work in the ages that pass.[2]

Most Vishnuvites (followers of Vishnu) accept ten such earthly Manifestations or Avatars. The last four are generally believed to be Rama, Krishna, Buddha, and Kalki or Kalkin who is yet to appear. Bahá'ís believe Bahá'u'lláh's appearance fulfilled the Vishnuvite expectations of Kalki.

Krishna's life

Attempts to reconstruct Krishna's life as a historical and divine figure reveal not one but several Krishnas. Various Hindu texts, ranging from the early Upanishads to the Mahabharata and the Puranas, mention Krishna. Generally, two essentially distinct and not easily reconcilable personalities appear out of the stories surrounding Him. In the Mahabharata, Krishna is a serious, severe, and resourceful war-hero. His divine power and wisdom, identical with that of Lord Vishnu Himself, enables Him to provide spiritual advice to His cousin, Prince Arjuna, who is about to enter a battle of good and evil. In Hindu thought, Arjuna is generally understood to be anyone seeking spiritual insight. The result of the captivating dialogue between Krishna and Arjuna is the masterpiece of Hindu sacred literature – the Bhagavad Gita (Song of the Blessed Lord).

In contrast, the Krishna of the Puranas is an indigenous cowherd, raised by village step-parents, who grows up to be a playful, flute-playing prankster. He spends his leisure with countless milkmaids (*gopis*) among whom the beautiful Radha is His favourite. The mischievous Krishna of the Puranas plays a pivotal role in the vast folklore of India.

The story of Krishna is thus a mixture of fact and fable. Some sources consider Him to be a mere legend, while others view Him as a real historical figure, born some time between 3,000 B.C.E. and 900 B.C.E. in Mathura, India. Some sources even provide details of His daily activities,[3] and His birth is celebrated to this day in Indian festivals:

> In August or September, Vaishnavites [Vishnuvites] celebrate Krishna's birthday *(Janmashtami).* At His birthplace, Mathura, Krishna's devotees fast and keep a

vigil until midnight, retelling stories of his life. In some places Krishna's image is placed in a cradle and lovingly rocked by devotees. Elsewhere, pots of milk, curds, and butter – playfully stolen by young Krishna – are strung high above the ground to be seized by young men who form human pyramids to get to their prize.[4]

The Bhagavad Gita's teachings and influence

Krishna's most significant contribution to the Hindu tradition is the Bhagavad Gita, one of the great classics of religious literature. Though the Gita is now often published as a separate work, it was originally a small part of the Mahabharata, the longest poem in the world, made up of 220,000 lines and compiled over a period of 800 years (400 B.C.E. to 400 C.E.). Since its composition over many centuries during the first millennium B.C.E., Gita has become the basic Hindu code of moral conduct. Countless generations, including great men such as Mahatma Gandhi (who considered the Gita to be his spiritual "mother" and whose selfless, non-violent approach was grounded in its noble principles), have been influenced by its moral teachings. Eventually, Gita's sphere of influence expanded beyond Hinduism to affect Buddhism, Jainism, and even Muslim Sufism.

Krishna's three Ways to salvation

In the Bhagavad Gita, Krishna identifies three ways in which humans can achieve salvation:

1. **The path of knowledge** *(Jnana marga)* appeals primarily to the intellectual mind. Krishna approves the advice in the Upanishads to practise yoga and meditation in order to gain insight into one's identity with Brahman, and so attain salvation.
2. **The way of disinterested action** *(Karma marga)* appeals to the legalistic mind who wants to achieve liberation by performing exact rituals, including sacrifices. Krishna confirms

that if these actions are performed with no attachment to rewards, they can bring liberation.

3. **The path of selfless devotion** *(Bhakti)* appeals to the general masses by inviting them to absolute dedication of the heart and mind to the Personal God (Ishvara). This path is the one most emphasized throughout the Gita. By showing selfless devotion to Krishna (the personification of Ishvara), "calling on His name, reciting praises of Him, and always keeping Him in mind," one can essentially take the shortest route to liberation, devoting one's life to the loving worship and service of Krishna with no eye on otherworldly rewards.[5] Serving Krishna is realized through service to others.

Unlike the other two paths, Bhakti is non-exclusive and open to members of both sexes, to all castes, and to righteous and unrighteous alike:

> Even if a very evil doer
> Reveres Me with single devotion
> He must be regarded as righteous in spite of all;
> For he has the right resolution.
>
> Quickly his soul becomes righteous,
> And he goes to eternal peace.
> Son of Kunti, make sure of this:
> No devotee of Mine is lost.
>
> For all those who come to me for shelter,
> However weak or humble or sinful they may be,
> Women or artisans, and servants
> They all reach the Path supreme.[6]

The Bhakti way (selfless love and devotion to a Hindu deity) is at the heart of the Gita. Nothing is more emphasized throughout this work. However, the Gita also teaches that the Lord returns this love by protecting human beings when they need it through His periodic reappearances in the world which restore righteousness and order in the cosmos. The Gita also teaches that the human soul (embodied self) is immortal:

> Our bodies are known to end, but the embodied self is enduring, indestructible, and immeasurable; therefore, Arjuna, fight the battle . . .
>
> It cannot be cut or burned; cannot be wet or withered; it is enduring, all-pervasive, fixed, immovable, and timeless.[7]

Among the most critical contributions of Krishna to Hindu thought was the modernization of Hindu philosophy by placing greater emphasis on monotheism, ethical behaviour, acquisition of knowledge, selfless action, and the value of service to others, while de-emphasizing traditional, ritualistic behaviour.

By converting the unknowable Brahman into a loving, caring God who deliberately intervenes in human affairs at critical junctures in history, Krishna made the Hindu religion much more practical and modern. While the average Hindu knew virtually nothing about Brahman, he learned a great deal about Him through the human/divine figure of Krishna. He could even engage in a dialogue with this personal God through Arjuna. The Gita also leaves little doubt that, as an incarnation of Lord Vishnu, Krishna is indeed the Vedic Brahman and represents the same qualifications, powers, and functions:

> I am the universal father, mother, granter of all, grandfather, object of knowledge, purifier, holy syllable OM, threefold sacred lore.
>
> I am the way, sustainer, lord, witness, shelter, refuge, friend, source, dissolution, stability, treasure, and unchanging seed.

> When devoted men sacrifice to other deities with faith, they sacrifice to me, Arjuna, however aberrant is the rites.
>
> Votaries of gods go to the gods, ancestor-worshippers go to ancestors, those who propitiate ghosts go to them, and my worshippers go to me.
>
> If they rely on me, Arjuna, women, commoners, men of low rank, even men born in womb of evil, reach the highest way.
>
> Keep me in your mind and devotion, sacrifice to me, bow to me, discipline yourself toward me, and you will reach me.[8]

For over 2,000 years, countless generations throughout the world have been inspired by Krishna's words. Today, His teachings affect virtually every aspect of Hindu life, and beyond that the lives of millions of others across the globe.

Zoroaster

Zoroaster is the founder of the ancient religion of Persia (Iran) known as Zoroastrianism. His original name, as mentioned in the Gathas (Songs), was Zarathushtra ("Golden Shining Star": according to linguists, Zar means "gold"; ushtra comes from ush meaning "shining"; and stra means "star"). Because the teachings of Zoroaster spread widely in different regions of the ancient world, other forms of His name also exist: Zoroaster in Greek, Zartosht in Persian, and Zardusht in Gujarati. The term Zarathustra is the combined form of Zarathushtra and Zoroaster. After Alexander the Great conquered Persia in 331 B.C.E., the names Zarathustra and Zardusht gave way to the Greek Zoroaster.

Neither the birth date nor the birthplace of Zoroaster can be established with certainty. Most Zoroastrian scholars believe that He was born some time between 1700 B.C.E. and 660 B.C.E. in the district of Azerbaijan near Lake Urumiah in northern Iran. According to later Zoroastrian sources, His mother was a 15-year-old virgin when she gave birth to Him. Five months into her pregnancy, Zoroaster's mother saw in a dream the impending destruction of the world. She was struck with fear, but in the dream an angel came to her and gave her the glad-tidings that she was bearing a great Prophet who would alter the course of events. According to some Zoroastrian texts, divine beings were present at Zoroaster's birth and the newborn baby smiled as He acknowledged the presence of these celestial beings.

Zoroaster came from a noble Persian family. He is primarily known through the Gathas, a small collection of hymns believed to have been composed by Him in Gathic, an ancient dialect closely related to the Vedic and pre-dating the Avestan language. The Gathas are still extant and faithfully preserved by the Zoroastrian community.

At the age of 20, Zoroaster left His parents' home and was divinely guided to a secluded place on Mount Ushidarena, also known as Ushidam (the abode of dawn, divine intellect). He stayed in the mountain recesses for a period of ten years. There, He devoted His time to prayer, meditation, and spiritual purification. His hymns suggest that the Prophet saw acts of violence, as the worshippers of the *daevas* (malevolent gods) pillaged peaceful communities, and slaughtered and carryed off cattle. Unable to stop these atrocities, Zoroaster became filled with a profound sense of justice and a deep yearning for peace and tranquility in the world. Zoroastrian tradition maintains that the Prophet lived at a time when immorality, oath-breaking, falsehood, and personal impurity characterized the people of His land.

At the age of 30, Zoroaster had the first of a series of visions that inspired Him to preach a new message. It was on the banks of the Daitya River in Azerbaijan – the Jordan of Zoroastrianism

– that a great shining being, the archangel Vohu Mana (Good Thought) appeared to Zoroaster. The archangel led the Prophet into the presence of Ahura Mazda (the Wise Lord, a term that signifies God in Zoroastrianism) and five other celestial beings in paradise. Later, the Prophet experienced the attributes (*amesha spentas*) of Ahura Mazda and held communion with the Wise Lord on many occasions.* In paradise, Zoroaster became fully acquainted with the empyrean realms and with the celestial hierarchy of God, the archangels, and the angels. He was also called to prophethood and instructed in the doctrines and duties of the new religion.

Following these visions, He began teaching the new message with fervent zeal but for ten years He experienced no success. His message was rejected, even ridiculed, by the priests and the religious leaders of the land. Even His own father was not on His side at beginning. Discouraged, He was tempted by the Evil Spirit (Angra Mainyu), who bade Him renounce the worship of the Wise Lord. However, Zoroaster did not yield to temptation and continued His divine work. At last, after ten years of effort, Zoroaster made His first convert – His cousin Maidhyoimah.

This conversion gave Him the courage to go to the court of the Aryan Prince Vishtaspa, who reigned over a distant region of eastern Persia. There, He began a two-year effort to win this ruler to the new religion. However, Vishtaspa was dominated by the Karapans, a greedy group of priests who were involved in animal sacrifices and magic. Zoroastrian tradition maintains that the priests, feeling threatened by Zoroaster's presence at court, planned a scheme to misrepresent Him as a sorcerer. They hid a variety of paraphernalia associated with witchcraft and sorcery, including the nails, hair, and heads of dogs and cats, in Zoroaster's dwelling. Upon the discovery of these, Zoroaster was cast into prison for two years. In the end, a miracle brought

* These visions of paradise bestowed upon Zoroaster resemble, to some degree, the seven heavens that Muhammad, the Prophet of Islam, experienced during His night journey (*mi'ráj*) to paradise.

about His freedom. While in prison, Zoroaster won the willing ear of the Vishtaspa by curing his favorite black horse of paralysis. This event marked a turning point in Zoroaster's fortunes and His mission; Vishtaspa decided to adopt the Zoroastrian faith. Soon more conversions followed, and Zoroaster's own family, relatives, and friends became faithful adherents.

Zoroaster is generally believed to have died at the age of 77, but accounts of His death vary. One frequently cited record notes that He and Lohrasp, the King of Persia (Vishtaspa's father) were killed together. They were engaged in prayer and meditation in an unprotected fire temple when the sworn enemy of the Empire, King Arjasp of the neighboring Turan, attacked the temple and killed the Prophet and the old King. According to this account, Zoroaster died of wounds from a javelin.

The influence of Zoroaster and of His teachings

Zoroaster's influence has so far gone largely unnoticed outside the circle of adherents and religious scholars. This is gradually beginning to change, though. The impact of His teachings, especially on Abrahamic religions, can hardly be denied. Zoroaster was the first to teach such fundamental religious doctrines as:

- individual judgment
- heaven and hell
- the future resurrection of the body
- the universal resurrection of humankind (Last Judgment)
- eternal life for the reunited soul and body

These doctrines later became familiar articles of faith for much of humanity through Judaism, Christianity and Islam.

Like Abraham, Zoroaster also taught monotheism. In the Gathas, Ahura Mazda, the Wise Lord, creates the universe through the agency of Spenta Mainyu (equivalent to the Holy Spirit). The people of Zoroaster's time believed in the existence of many ahuras and daevas, ahuras being evil spirits and daevas good spirits. Zoroaster reversed this model and made ahuras good spirits and daevas evil spirits. He placed Ahura Mazda at the top of the hierarchy of ahuras as the possessor of all good attributes.

Ahura Mazda expresses Himself through good spirits or lesser ahuras whose names reflect the virtues of the Wise Lord that His followers are to aspire to. Whether these spirits are simply aspects of Ahura Mazda or independent celestial beings is not clear in the Gathas. The most important of them is the Holy Spirit (*Spenta Mainyu*), who is the agent of creation. Others represent power, devotion, immortality and obedience. Zoroastrians are encouraged to be among those who renew the world and help it progress towards perfection (Gathas 30: 9). We find tantalizing similarities between these Zoroastrian concepts and those in later Jewish mystical literature of the Kabbalah, in Christian gnosticism, and in some of the New Testament letters.

The Three Wise Men

There is some evidence that the three Wise Men (Magi) who heralded the infant Jesus were in fact Zoroastrians. Matthew notes that the Wise Men came from the east and brought the infant Jesus gifts of gold, frankincense, and myrrh. To this day, frankincense and myrrh are offered at the altars of Zoroastrian temples. The frankincense which Jewish and Christian authors interpret as a symbol of honor to the divinity of Christ is also part of Zoroastrian worship. Known as loban, frankincense is sprinkled on the embers of the Zoroastrian Sacred Fire as a fragrant homage to the bright symbol of Ahura Mazda.

What were the three Wise Men searching for? One idea held by some is that they were searching for the Zoroastrian Savior *Saoshyant* (Benefactor of Humankind), an ideal king or savior expected by the Persians and similar in character and mission to the Messiah awaited by the Jews.

Moses

The origins of Judaism go back to the time of Abraham, who is considered to be the father of monotheism in the Judeo-Christian tradition. The Hebrew Bible (Old Testament) relates that the God of Abraham, El, commanded Him to migrate with His family from Ur of the Chaldees to the land of Canaan, later known as Palestine. This migration took place some time between 2000 and 1700 B.C.E. There, He received the following revelation from God:

> I am the Lord that brought thee out of Ur of the Chaldees to give to thee this land to inherit.[9]

After Abraham's death, His son Isaac and grandson Jacob succeeded Him. A terrible famine forced Jacob and his family to migrate to the borders of Egypt. Jacob had twelve sons who, as the Hebrew population began to grow, became the heads of the twelve tribes of Israel. For several centuries, the Israelites led a quiet life in and around Egypt. However, their growing number and influence began to alarm the Egyptians. This led the Pharaoh Ramses II, who had a passion for building large cities and monumental temples and was looking for unpaid labor, to enslave the Israelites. To further stop the growth of the Hebrew population, and as a precaution against the Hebrews joining forces in wartime with enemies of Egypt, the Pharaoh decided to have all the Hebrew boys of his generation thrown into the Nile River.

Moses was born during these perilous times. His mother kept Him hidden for three months at home, but at last, fearful that an enemy might discover the child, she decided to take a calculated risk. She knew that Moses had virtually no chance of survival while in an Israelite home, and so she put the baby into a waterproof basket made of reeds and sent Him floating down the Nile River, hoping that along the way an Egyptian family might discover Him and decide to raise Him as one of their own. As fate would have it, the basket drifted toward the Pharaoh's palace. Moses was found by Pharaoh's daughter, who had no children of her own and decided to adopt the baby and raise Him in the palace as an Egyptian prince.

When He had grown to manhood and become aware of His heritage, Moses one day saw an Egyptian beating an Israelite, one of His people. Overcome by a sudden outburst of rage, He attacked the Egyptian and killed him. This event irrevocably altered His destiny. The following day He fled eastward to the land of Midian, where He joined the household of Jethro, a Midianite priest. Eventually He married Jethro's daughter Zipporah, with whom He had two sons.

Jewish tradition maintains that Moses was chosen by God to lead the Israelites out of Egypt. This divine appointment occurred one night when Moses was tending the flock of His father-in-law Jethro, on Mount Sinai. There He experienced the presence of an angel from God amidst a bush that burned but was not consumed. This event not only changed His own life but proved to alter the fate of the Israelites in Egypt. Through the angel, God declared that His new name was Yahweh and commanded Moses to lead his people out of an Egypt that had enslaved them, and to take them back to Canaan, the land of their ancestors.

When Moses returned to Egypt, He found the Pharaoh indifferent to His pleas. Directed by Yahweh, He first threatened and then, through divine intervention, struck Egypt with nine successive plagues. The tenth and final plague resulted in the death of all the first-born sons of the Egyptians, including the Pharaoh's. But the Hebrew families were "passed over" by the angel of death: during that terrible night they ate a sacred meal of roasted lamb, unleavened bread and bitter herbs, and marked their door posts with the blood of the lamb as a sign of their identity, so that the angel of death would not strike them. This final blow forced the Pharoah to reconsider, and he agreed to allow the Israelites to leave Egypt. But no sooner had they left than Pharaoh changed his mind and became intent on bringing his Hebrew slaves back. Jewish tradition holds that divine intervention prevented Pharaoh from attaining this goal. As they reached the Red (or Reed) Sea, the Israelites appeared to be trapped; Pharaoh and his army were closing in on them, while ahead of them lay the sea. According to tradition, God miraculously parted the waters of the sea so that the Israelites could pass through safely on a dry seabed. When the Egyptians reached the place and tried to follow the Israelites, the waters returned and they were all trapped and drowned.

Having crossed the Red Sea, the Hebrews came to Mount Sinai on their way to Canaan. Tradition maintains that Moses left His people at the foot of the mountain and went up to commune with the Lord. Forty days later, He came back with two stone tablets that He announced had been delivered to him by Yahweh. The tablets had the new Israelite code of conduct inscribed on them: the Ten Commandments.

During Moses' absence, however, the Israelites, under the reluctant supervision of His brother Aaron, had reverted to the practice of idol-worship, explicitly forbidden by Yahweh. They had melted down their gold jewelry and cast it into the shape of a golden calf. Upon His return, Moses became so outraged by their idolatry that He smashed the two stone tablets into the golden calf and destroyed both the calf and the tablets. Yet He interceded with Yahweh to forgive the sins and weakness of the Israelites.

He then went back to Mount Sinai for another forty days, during which He communed with God and then brought back a new set of stone tablets, engraved with the Ten Commandments. After these divine encounters, Moses' face is said to have been so bright that He had to use a veil. Tradition maintains that, at the bidding of Yahweh, the Israelites constructed a portable shrine called the Tabernacle of God. Within this Tabernacle stood a chest or box containing the stone tablets marked with the Ten Commandments. This box later became known as the Ark of the Covenant. As the Israelites continued their journey to the promised land of Canaan, Moses used the privacy of this portable shrine to hold communion with God.

When Moses and His people reached the borders of Canaan (Palestine) at last, He told them that it was Yahweh's will that they should invade and capture this land. But the Israelites lost courage and rebelled against both Moses and Yahweh. This angered Yahweh, and so in divine retribution the Hebrews were condemned to wander in the wilderness for the next forty years. At last, the main body of the Hebrew tribes approached the cultivated lands of Canaan. It was granted to Moses to look over to the Promised Land, but He was not permitted to enter it — once again sacrificing Himself for the sins of His people.

The story of Moses is not mentioned in non-Semitic sources. According to the Hebrew Bible, He passed away at the age of 120. The narratives of the Bible were probably written from four to six hundred years after His time.

Gautama Buddha

Information about the life of Buddha (the Enlightened One) is sketchy. His teachings, often given in sermons, were not collected in written form until about four hundred years after His death. In the meantime, Buddha's teachings were preserved, added to and memorized by Buddhist monks, but only a few factual details of His life are available today. The idea of writing the life story of Buddha was perhaps the farthest thing from the minds of His disciples at the time; their main interest was in receiving enlightenment from their Master.

The earliest written details of Buddha's life appear several centuries after His passing. The sources available to the authors of these early biographies contained a hard-to-decipher mixture of legend and factual information. At times, some of these accounts give as many as four different versions of a single event in Buddha's life. Many of these stories, while rich in symbolism and moral and ethical content, cannot be attributed with certainty to the person of Gautama Buddha.

Buddha was born around 563 B.C.E. near the town of Kapilavastu in what is now the country of Nepal. His father, Suddhodana (Pure Rice) was probably a wealthy landowner who served as one of the chieftains of the Kshatriya caste of the Shakya clan. According to Buddhist legend, Buddha's conception was immaculate, His birth was virgin and His body bore all the marks of a universal monarch. His mother, Maya, is believed to have dreamed that the future Buddha came to her in the form of a white elephant and entered her womb. The Brahmins' (Hindu priests) interpretation of her dream was that a son would be born to Maya who would become either the king of India or an enlightened monk who would share His awakening with the world.

At his birth Buddha was given the name Siddartha, meaning "he who has reached his goal." His family name was Gautama. Legend maintains that Siddartha's father, Suddhodana, in the hope of encouraging his son to embrace His royal future, tried his best to make Buddha's life so pleasant that He would not think of retiring from it. Buddhist texts describe His early life as a happy and joyous time full of kingly luxuries — from white umbrellas for shade, to fine clothes, perfumes, a palace for each season, a harem of dancing girls, and the company of female musicians. At the age of 16, He is said to have married Yasodhara, a princess, who bore Him a son, Rahula.

Despite His father's orders that He stay in His palaces, on three occasions the adventurous Siddartha mounted His chariot and rode out into the world where He encountered what He later identified as the three inescapable evils afflicting the human race: old age, sickness, and death. Venturing out of His palace a fourth time, He saw their remedy: the peace and tranquility of a mendicant ascetic. Then one night, at the age of 29, in the spirit of Indian renunciation, He bade an unspoken farewell to His sleeping wife and son. Departing from His luxurious home, He shaved His head, exchanged His rich garments for the coarse yellow robe, and assumed the life of a wandering beggar. The gentle and kind-hearted Siddartha was now on a mission to solve the riddle of life. For the next six years, He struggled to find a solution to the dilemma of human suffering that was so pervasive in His surroundings.

First, He studied with two yoga masters, Alara Kalama and Uddaka, striving through constant yoga exercises to unite His soul (*atman*) with Brahman, the Universal Soul. But when their teachings did not lead Him to true knowledge, Siddartha turned to extreme asceticism. Accompanied by five Hindu holy men, He tried various techniques of self-denial such as exposure to extreme heat and cold, a bed of brambles, breath retention and severe reduction of food until, on the verge of starvation, He became dreadfully emaciated. Realizing the uselessness of such extreme asceticism, He accepted an offering of rice from a village woman and ate it. The five holy men saw in this gesture of Gautama a proof of weakness and left Him in disgust.

Sitting under a fig tree, the sacred Bodhi tree at Bodh-gaya in northeast India, He vowed that He would not leave that spot until He received awakening. According to the legend, the armies of the Tempter Mara (the personification of evil) attacked Him with storms, rain, rocks, and blazing weapons. Mara offered Siddhartha the wealth of the world if He would give up His mission. Yet Gautama sat unmoved. At dawn, He defeated Mara, thus becoming the Buddha or "Enlightened One", in possession of the solution (the Four Noble Truths) to the age-old dilemma of human suffering, and the road-map (the Noble Eightfold Path) to *nirvana*, freedom from suffering.

The Four Noble Truths are as follows: 1) Sorrow is universal; 2) The cause of sorrow is attachment; 3) To overcome sorrow, one needs to overcome attachment; 4) To do so, one must follow the Noble Eightfold Path: right knowledge, right intention, right speech, right conduct, right means of livelihood, right effort, right mindfulness, right concentration.

Buddha first shared His newly-found enlightenment with the same five ascetics who had abandoned Him earlier. He did this in a park outside Benares. All five accepted His teaching; on that day, the Buddhist monastic order called Sangha came into being.

For the next forty-five years Buddha traveled widely throughout the northern Indian countryside, giving numerous sermons and winning the allegiance of people of all sects and classes. Some of His followers became monks (*bhikkhus*), emulating Buddha's life of poverty and spiritual dedication, while others continued as householders. Buddha's own father Suddhodana became a lay disciple, while His son Rahula joined the order of monks. Buddha's wife Yasodhara and His stepmother joined the order of nuns (*bhikkunis*).

Buddha died at about the age of 80. His death was apparently the result of eating some indigestible food – either poisonous mushrooms or tainted pork. As His monks gathered around Him to pay their last respects, Buddha uttered His final words on the impermanence of all things and exhorted them to work out their salvation with strong determination. Having said these words, He passed on to Nirvana, the end of all suffering.

Jesus Christ

Our information about the life of Jesus comes primarily from the four Gospels of Matthew, Mark, Luke and John, and a few additional references in other books of the New Testament. The exact date of the birth of Jesus is not known. According to the Gospel of Matthew, He was born during the reign of Herod the Great. Since Herod died in 4 B.C.E., most scholars believe that Jesus was born no later than 6 or 7 B.C.E. The details of His birth are found only in the Gospels of Matthew and Luke, who note that He was of the lineage of David and was born in the city of Bethlehem (the native town of David) even though His parents lived in Nazareth.

According to Matthew and Luke, Jesus was conceived by the Holy Spirit and born of a virgin mother – Mary, who was married to a carpenter named Joseph. Luke states that Mary and Joseph had to journey to the city of Bethlehem to satisfy a Roman ruling that everyone should go to their ancestral cities for a census. When Jesus' parents arrived at Bethlehem, they could not find a room at the inn, so Mary, who was about to give birth, had to find shelter in a stable. Here the child was born, and was cradled in the manger of a donkey. The baby was named Jesus, which means "God saves." Luke recounts that a group of Bethlehem shepherds, to whom a host of angels had appeared with the glad-tidings of the birth of a savior, came to pay their respects to the newborn Jesus. Matthew, on the other hand, speaks of "the wise men from the east" who followed a star and arrived at Bethlehem to pay homage to the child, bringing Him gifts of gold, frankincense and myrrh.

The Gospels do not shed much light on the childhood and youth of Jesus. His parents were perhaps quietly religious. This can be inferred from Luke, who mentions that Mary and Joseph traveled to the city of Jerusalem each year to observe the Passover, rather than doing so in their native Bethlehem. Over time, Jesus became familiar enough with the Hebrew Bible to freely quote passages from that Book. Soon, He became so proficient in Jewish Law that, according to Luke, He entered a heated religious debate with some Jewish rabbis in the Jerusalem Temple when He was a mere lad of 12. Evidently, Jesus astonished the rabbis with the depth and breadth of His Biblical knowledge.

Joseph trained Jesus to become a carpenter. Yet His future calling left Jesus only a brief period of time to practise that profession. Mark maintains (6: 3) that Jesus grew up in a large family of seven: Jesus, James, Joses, Jude, Simon, and two unnamed sisters. But after describing the above-mentioned debate in the Temple, the New Testament has virtually no information on the next eighteen years of Jesus' life. Most Biblical scholars believe that, during these "silent years" Joseph died and Jesus, as the eldest son, took over the management of His father's carpentry business, with His brothers helping Him.

According to all the four Gospels, Jesus was baptized at the age of 30 by His cousin, John the Baptist, in the River Jordan. John was a desert prophet, perhaps from the peaceful and reclusive Qumran community of the Essenes. The Essenes were one of several Jewish sects of the time whose ideology and practices were in sharp contrast to the extreme views of the Zealots to which militants such as Barabbas belonged. John proclaimed God's wrath on the Jews, calling on them to mend their ways rather than depend for salvation on their Abrahamic lineage. He also prophesied that One greater than himself would soon appear as the agent of God's judgment. He saw that figure to be his cousin, Jesus.

The Gospels state that people from all parts of Palestine came to hear this desert ascetic and to be baptized by him. Baptism was both a pagan and a Jewish practice. Some Jewish sects (including the Essenes) baptized Gentile converts to Judaism. John, however, had the revolutionary idea of extending the practice of baptism to Jews themselves. Immersing oneself in water had symbolic connotations; for John it signified the washing away of Jewish sins and preparing the people for the impending arrival of their savior, the expected Messiah.

Matthew (3: 16) reports that Jesus was among the Jews seeking baptism by John in the Jordan river. Following the ceremony, as he stepped out of the river, the Holy Spirit appeared to him in the form of a dove and addressed him as His beloved son. To most Christians, this signifies the event that ushered in the active ministry of Jesus. For the forty days following His baptism, Jesus retired into the wilderness and engaged in periodic fasting, prayer, and meditation. Matthew (4: 1-11) notes that in the wilderness, Satan tried to tempt Jesus to use His spiritual power for secular ends, but Jesus refused to do so.*

In contrast to Matthew, John's Gospel recounts that the baptism of Jesus was followed by the gathering of His first disciples. Christian tradition maintains that the apostles, Jesus' initial band of disciples, were twelve in number. The fisherman Simon, called Peter, was the first apostle. Among the other apostles were James and John, sons of Zebedee (also fishermen), Nathanael, Thomas, Judas Iscariot, and Matthew, a tax collector. These twelve, however, were not the only early disciples of Jesus.

The majority of His own people, however, were quick to reject His claims. Some, such as the Zealots who sought the violent overthrow of the Roman Empire, scorned at such pacifist remarks by Jesus as "turning the other cheek" to the enemy. Jesus also alienated the Sadducees, another Jewish group, by claiming that human beings had an immortal soul, a principle the Sadducees vehemently rejected. Of all Jewish groups, perhaps the Pharisees had the most in common with Jesus. Yet while Jesus agreed with the Pharisees that the Jews should observe the Jewish Law, He vastly differed from them as to what constituted observance of that Law. The Pharisees were devoted to strict observance of all the accretions to the Jewish Law made over the centuries by the rabbis, such as the prohibition of eating an egg laid on the Sabbath. To Jesus the *spirit* of the Law took precedence over the *letter*. He thus offended the Pharisees and scribes by openly attacking them for their narrow legalistic and inflexible views on authority, the Torah, taxes, divorce, resurrection, and the like. His main enemies, as with all major Prophets, were the religious leaders of His time and place, to whom He was an imposter and a deceiver.

While the New Testament does not give an exact duration for the ministry of Jesus, internal Biblical evidence suggests that His entire ministry lasted anywhere from a little over two

* Similar accounts of temptation by Satan or demonic forces are found in Zoroastrian and Buddhist sacred literature, as we have seen.

years to around three and a half years (e.g., see Luke 3: 21-22; Luke 4: 1-15; John 2: 13; John 6: 4; and John 13: 1).

The Gospels report that Jesus knew that His opponents would soon put Him to death and He had prepared Himself for it. He even warned His disciples that their lives would also be in danger as they carried on His work. Jesus not only foresaw His death, but knew that one of His own disciples would betray Him. Sharing a last meal with His inner circle in Jerusalem during the Passover, He performed a ceremony with bread and wine and asked those present to continue to perform that ceremony from then on, as a symbolic and mystical way of communing with Him. It was during this Last Supper that Jesus shocked His disciples by claiming that one of them would soon betray Him to the hostile Jewish authorities. That disciple, Judas Iscariot, had in fact already done so, by selling information leading to Jesus' arrest for 30 pieces of silver.

That evening, Jesus took three of His disciples to the Garden of Gethsemane on the Mount of Olives. There, while the disciples slept, He prayed intensely that should it be God's Will, the cup of suffering would pass away from Him. That was not meant to be, however. Later that night, an armed band of Jewish priests and elders, led by Judas, approached Jesus with swords and clubs and brought Him before the high priest Caiaphas. Caiaphas tried to establish Jesus as a blasphemer by asking Him several theological questions. One was regarding Jesus' claim to be the Son of the living God. According to the Gospel of Matthew, Jesus answered:

> You have said: nevertheless, I say unto you, 'Hereafter shall ye see the Son of man sitting on the right hand of power, and coming in the clouds of heaven.[10]

The high priest considered this statement to be blasphemy, and Jesus was pronounced deserving of death. Since the priests were unable to carry out the sentence without the consent of the Roman authorities, Jesus was brought before Pontius Pilate, the Roman governor of Jerusalem. Following a brief interrogation during which he could find no fault in Jesus, Pilate (as was his custom during the Passover) offered the Jewish crowd in his courtyard the release of one Jewish prisoner: either the pacifist Jesus, or the militant Barabbas, who in an insurrection had killed a Roman guard. The crowd chose Barabbas and called for Jesus' death by crucifixion, a form of punishment preceded by scourging and usually reserved for slaves, revolutionaries, and common criminals.

Accordingly, Jesus was first scourged, then crowned with thorns, and finally forced to carry His own cross to the place of His execution – a hill called Golgotha (the place of a skull). There, He was nailed to a cross between two thieves. His ordeal lasted for about six hours. Then, in the words of the first verse of the twenty-second Psalm, He cried out, "My God, My God, why hast thou forsaken me?" and passed away.

The crucifixion of Jesus is believed to have taken placed on a Friday some time between 27 and 33 C.E. That same day, Joseph of Arimathea, a wealthy and well-respected Jewish counsellor – and a secret disciple of Jesus – asked Pilate for the body of Jesus, had it wrapped in a linen shroud, and placed in his own empty tomb.

The Gospels recount that, two days later, Mary Magdalene and other women believers went to the tomb and, to their amazement, found it empty. Jesus then appeared to the disciples on several occasions, comforting them and exhorting them to teach in His name. Luke and John, particularly, viewed these events as a sign of the physical resurrection of Jesus, and eventually their views were adopted by the Church Fathers. However, there is no agreement even among Christians as to how to interpret the phenomenon of the missing body of Jesus, the empty tomb, and the appearance of Jesus to His disciples. Followers who take a literal stand on Luke and John's accounts believe that Jesus overcame death and that His body was physically resurrected and lifted up to the heavens. To them, this event is at the heart of Christian theology and cosmology, establishing the divinity of Jesus as the only person in history to defeat death. It also confers on Jesus the unique ability to restore life to other mortals and bestow upon them eternal life.[11] This He will do upon His return to earth, when He will establish an eternal kingdom by raising the dead from among His past fold (Christians) and, once and for all, end all physical death.

However, other passages in the New Testament, particularly those by the Apostle Paul, seem to hint that the empty tomb has a symbolic significance, and that the phenomenon of the Resurrection should be viewed as a spiritual event with profound mystical meaning. For instance, in the first Epistle to the Corinthians, Paul equates his own vision of Jesus on the way to Damascus with those of the disciples at the time of the Resurrection (I Cor. 15: 1-8), and then (15: 42-45) he claims that in his vision he saw the *spiritual*, not the physical, body of Jesus. Thus he implies that what the disciples experienced and told others about was the *spiritual* body of Jesus, as the physical body of their Master, made of flesh and blood, could not share in the kingdom of God:

> It is so with the resurrection of the dead. The body is sown in decay, it is raised free from decay. . . It is a physical body that is sown, it is a spiritual body that is raised . . . I can tell you this brothers: flesh and blood can not share in the kingdom of God, and decay will not share in what is imperishable.[12]

Over time, the disciples' post-crucifixion experiences of their Master transformed their utter disillusionment and despair into hope, confidence, and renewed faith. With newfound resolve, they began spreading Christ's message of love, tolerance, and brotherhood throughout different regions.

The example of Jesus' sacrificial life and death, as well as His divine teachings, set in motion an irreversible process of transformation in human character that changed forever the spiritual fortunes of hundreds of millions. Today, Christianity is the most widespread religion in the world with close to two billion followers.

Muhammad

Muhammad ("the Praised One") is the Prophet-founder of the religion of Islam. The title of the religion means "submission", which implies submission to the will of God. Born about 570 C.E. in the city of Mecca in today's Saudi Arabia, Muhammad was from the Hashimite clan of the Quraysh tribe. The clan's founder Hashim traced his lineage back to Ishmael, son of Abraham. Muhammad's infancy and childhood were marked by tragedy. His father 'Abd'u'lláh died before Muhammad was born and His mother Amina passed away when He was six. For the next two years, Muhammad's grandfather 'Abdu'l-Muṭṭalib took care of Him. When this grandfather died, Muhammad came under the care of His uncle 'Abú Tálib, who was involved with the caravan trade constantly crossing the Arabian desert. According to Muslim tradition, while Muhammad was accompanying His uncle to Syria on a caravan at the age of only 12, He met a Christian monk called Bahíráh who recognized Him as a future Prophet.

Muhammad's honesty earned Him the title of *al-Amín* (Trustworthy). He was soon entrusted with the leadership of many caravans. At the age of 25, He married a wealthy widow named Khadijah, whose caravans He had in His charge. Although Khadijah was fifteen years older than Muhammad, the two enjoyed a close relationship for years to come. They had two sons (who died in infancy) and four daughters, one of whom was named Fatimah and married Muhammad's cousin 'Alí, who with his descendants was to become a focal point of the Shi'i branch of Islam.

Before He was called to prophethood, Muhammad used to withdraw regularly to a cave on Mount Hirá, a few miles north of the city of Mecca. There, in the solitude of the cave, He engaged in meditation and contemplation. Perhaps He also sought insight into the social ills that had engulfed His environment – from senseless bloodshed and intertribal anarchy to rampant drinking, gambling, polytheism, and the inhuman practice of some Arab tribes of burying unwanted female infants alive. Around the age of 40, while meditating in the cave one night – later known to Muslims as the night of Qadr (Power and Excellence) – Muhammad received the first of a series of revelations from God. The Archangel Gabriel appeared to Him in a vision and commanded Him to recite. Muhammad answered that He had nothing to recite, for He was unlettered. Twice Gabriel repeated the command, and each time the bewildered and frightened Muhammad pleaded that He did not know what to say. At the third command, He was able to recite the first words of what later became the sacred text of the Islamic dispensation – the Qur'án. The name of this holy Book has been variously translated as "Book," "Read," or "Recite:"

> RECITE thou, in the name of thy Lord who created
> Created man from CLOTS OF BLOOD
>
> RECITE thou! For thy Lord is the most beneficent
> Who hath taught the use of the pen
> Who had taught man that which he knoweth not.[12]

Islamic tradition states that Muhammad reacted to His call to prophethood in much the same manner as the Jewish prophets – with fear and doubt. For a while, He remained shocked by this mysterious experience, fearing that He might have been possessed by spirits (*jinns*). In popular Arab belief, soothsayers and poets of Muhammad's era were thought to have been inspired by spirits, and the Prophet seems to have been in doubt as to whether the voice He heard came from a heavenly messenger or from a jinn. Deeply shaken, He returned home to His wife Khadijah, who comforted Him and reassured Him that He was not possessed. Later, she took Him for advice to her Christian cousin Waraqa bin Naufal, who had some knowledge of the Bible. Having heard Muhammad, Waraqa said that the same angel that had descended upon Moses had now descended upon Muhammad.

Muhammad nevertheless went through a period of self-questioning which lasted for several months. However, when verses continued to flow effortlessly from His lips, the unlettered Muhammad became convinced that God had indeed chosen him as a mouthpiece and that the verses He uttered were divine revelations. Muhammad also came to the conclusion that God had conferred upon him the station of Prophet (*nabi*) and Apostle of God (*rasul*). First, He quietly shared the new message with His inner circle of relatives and friends. His wife Khadijah was the first to accept the new call, followed by 'Alí, His cousin and future son-in-law. Muhammad's adopted son Zaid and future father-in-law Abu Bakr, who later succeeded Muhammad as the first Caliph of Islam, were also among the early converts.

At first, none but His immediate family heeded the new call. When Muhammad began to publicly preach the new message, He confronted hostility and ridicule. He insisted that His people should give up idol worship and strive to restore the monotheistic religion of Abraham, and because of this they rose against Him. They called Him a madman, a crazed poet, and began to persecute Him and His small band of followers. His neighbors threw stones into His house, injured His head, and scattered thorns outside His door. His greatest enemies came from His own tribe, the Quraysh, who unsuccessfully plotted to murder Him.

Over the next ten years, He continued to struggle in Mecca with little success. At the center of hostilities was the Umayyad clan of the Quraysh tribe, who later gave allegiance to the Prophet but whose descendants continued to challenge the family of Muhammad for generations to come. As conditions deteriorated in Mecca, the Prophet sent a number of His followers to Christian Abyssinia for safety.

Muslim tradition holds that at the height of His trials in Mecca, the Prophet was taken one night up to paradise and entered the presence of God. This journey is known as the Night Journey to Paradise (*mi'raj*). On that eventful night Muhammad, accompanied by the Archangel Gabriel, was taken through air, first to Jerusalem and then up through the seven heavens. As He passed through each heaven, He met holy figures of the past such as Adam, Enoch, Aaron, Moses, John the Baptist, Jesus, and Abraham. In the seventh heaven, He entered Paradise and attained the presence of God.

The year 620 C.E. marked a significant change in Muhammad's fortunes. He was invited by a delegation from Medina, a city to the north of Mecca, to serve as a main arbitrator in a long-standing feud among certain Arab tribes. Still despised in Mecca by the Quraysh, Muhammad and two hundred of His followers left Mecca secretly. This migration (*hijrah*) from Mecca to Medina occurred in June 622. The significance of the hijrah can be seen in its adoption as the beginning of the Muslim calendar, since it marked the change from persecution to appreciation of Muhammad and His followers. In Medina, the Prophet succeeded both in subduing the bitter feuds between the contending tribes and in establishing a brotherly unity among His Meccan fellow immigrants and the native Medinese. His house in Medina soon became a home and the first mosque (place of worship) in the history of Islam.

The nascent religion rapidly began to develop its own culture, with unique practices that included weekly services on Fridays, prostration during prayers, a call to prayer from the roof of the mosque, and the taking up of alms (*zakát*) for the poor and needy and for the support of the Muslim Faith.

Yet the hostility between the Meccans and their native Prophet now residing in Medina continued for nearly a decade.

At long last, in 630 C.E. Muhammad marched to Mecca with 10,000 men. The city, whose trade routes had been closed by the Muslims, surrendered, and the Prophet granted a general amnesty to His sworn enemies, excepting only a few.

Then He set out for the Ka'bah, a sanctuary believed to have been dedicated to God by Adam and containing the sacred Black Stone.[14] The sanctuary is said to have been rebuilt several times through the ages, including by Abraham. God had commanded Abraham to call His people to pilgrimage to this ancient house (*al-bayt al-'atiq*). Over time, the pagan Arabs had added their own "gods" to the sanctuary. Muhammad, who was intent on restoring monotheism among the Arabs, entered the Ka'bah, kissed the Black Stone, and then mounted His horse and rode seven times around the shrine as a sign of respect for the sanctuary, thus establishing the rites of pilgrimage (*hajj*) carried out by Muslims ever since. He then restored the lost monotheism to the sanctuary by ordering the destruction of the idols within it. This event established His political and religious ascendancy in Mecca once and for all.

Over the next two years, the previously warring tribes of Arabia came to universally embrace Islam. A new theocracy was established in the region, governed by the will of God. Tribal loyalties were transferred to a more inclusive religious loyalty that made brothers out of sworn enemies.

The Prophet died two years after the cleansing of the Ka'bah, in 632 C.E., but His followers marched on and ultimately conquered parts of three continents. They steadily built a civilization marked by great advancements in arts, sciences, and literature that put them far ahead of their European counterparts for many centuries.

Today, Islam is practised in all continents of the globe. Yet, particularly with the recent rise of Islamic fundamentalism, which prominently manifested itself in the September 11th terrorist attacks in the United States, the historical portrayal of Islam as a religion of violence and holy wars has been further reinforced in western societies. The media, and thus many people, have come to regard the militant Islam of Osama Bin Laden and the Taliban as the genuine face of Islam. In reality, though, these extremist movements and their violent tactics that are often based on ahistorical, exclusivist interpretations of certain Qur'anic passages are part of a larger internal struggle for the soul of Islam. A minority of dangerous, fanatical extremists in the Muslim world are dominating the media coverage against a majority of peaceful believers, ranging from conservatives to moderates, reformists, and liberals, who abhor the association of their Faith with senseless acts of terror. Islam may now be going through the same type of internal dissent and protestantism that Christianity experienced in the Middle Ages.

The Báb and Bahá'u'lláh

Bahá'u'lláh, an Arabic word meaning "Glory of God", is the title of the Prophet-founder of the Bahá'í Faith, the latest of the world religions. Bahá'u'lláh was born on 12 November 1817 in Tehran, the capital of Persia (Iran). His given name was Mírzá Ḥusayn-'Alí. His father, Mírzá Buzurg-í-Nurí, was a nobleman and a favored minister of Fath-'Alí Sháh, the King of Persia. His mother was Khadíjih Khánum. Bahá'u'lláh could trace His ancestry back to Abraham through the latter's third wife Katuráh, as well as to the ancient Persian Prophet Zoroaster. He was also a descendant of Yazdigird, the last king of the Sassanians, one of the great dynasties of Iran's imperial past.

According to Bahá'í writings, from childhood Bahá'u'lláh manifested signs of innate knowledge and unusual nobility of character. He led the princely life of a young aristocrat, receiving an education that focused mainly on swordsmanship, horsemanship, classical poetry, the study of the Qur'án, and calligraphy. In October 1835 He married Ásíyih Khánum, who like Himself came from a noble and wealthy family. They had three children, one of whom, 'Abbás (titled 'Abdu'l-Bahá or Servant of Glory), was later designated by Bahá'u'lláh as His successor and the sole interpreter of His teachings. When Bahá'u'lláh was 22 years old His father died, and the government wished Him to take over the position His father had enjoyed at court, as was customary in Persia at the time. But Bahá'u'lláh declined the offer and chose instead to devote His time and energy to a range of charitable activities that eventually earned Him widespread renown as the "Father of the Poor."

We now move back twenty years. When Bahá'u'lláh was about two years old, a child named Siyyíd 'Alí-Muhammad, who later became known to history as the Báb (meaning "Gate" in Arabic), was born on 20 October 1819 in southern Persia to a family of merchants. This child's parents were descendants of the Prophet Muhammad, as the title Siyyíd indicates. According to the surviving accounts, the Báb, like Bahá'u'lláh, was an extraordinary child.

Even though the Báb received only nominal training in reading and writing, He manifested such innate wisdom as to astonish those who came into contact with Him, including His teacher who, according to some accounts, later became one of His followers. The Báb's spiritual nature as a young boy inclined Him to spend long periods of time in meditation and prayer.

On 23 May 1844, the Báb announced a new revelation from God that would usher in a long-awaited era of justice, righteousness, and peace. Having assumed the title of "Báb" (Gate), He also announced that He was the Gate through which the Universal Messenger of God anticipated by the different religions of the past would soon appear. According to Bahá'ís, the role of the Báb in their history may in this respect be compared to that of John the Baptist in Christianity. As John prepared the way for the advent of Jesus, so in the same way the Báb prepared His followers for the coming of Bahá'u'lláh. However, for Bahá'ís the Báb is also an independent Manifestation of God with His own dispensation, ordinances, and teachings.

After this announcement, the Báb attracted many followers who called themselves Bábís. As His fame spread rapidly throughout the land, the government of Persia and the Muslim clergy, who saw the new movement as a threat to their own power and authority, began a systematic campaign of terror and persecution against Him and His followers. Thousands of Bábís – men, women, and children – were put to death as heretics in the most barbaric fashion. The news of these atrocities and the heroism of the Bábí martyrs in the face of horrifying persecution reached Europe and became the talk of educated people there.

The government finally decided to take aim at the root of the movement by executing the Báb, who had spent most of His ministry in prison in northern Persia. On 9 July 1850, He and one of His disciples who refused to be separated from Him were brought to the courtyard of the Tabriz army barracks to be executed in front of thousands of spectators. Though the firing squad consisted of many soldiers, the Báb and His disciple miraculously emerged unscathed from the first execution attempt. A second regiment had to be brought in, because the first regiment refused to repeat the execution. This time, both the Báb and His disciple were killed.

Bahá'u'lláh had accepted the Bábí Faith when He was 27 years old. The Báb had sent one of his followers to Tehran to personally deliver a sample of His Writings to Him. On reading these Writings, Bahá'u'lláh immediately recognized the station of the Báb. Since the Báb spent most of His days incarcerated in prison, Bahá'u'lláh soon became one of the outstanding figures of the young religion and it was under His leadership that the Bábís came to fully understand that a new religious dispensation had dawned.

Two years after the execution of the Báb, two young Bábís attempted to assassinate the King of Persia in an act of revenge. Half-demented and lacking sound judgment, they charged their pistols with pellets that were more suitable for killing birds than humans. Following this failed assassination attempt, not only were the two assailants killed, but many well-known Bábís were arrested and executed. Bahá'u'lláh severely condemned the assassination attempt, but was arrested and brought in chains to Tehran, the capital of Persia, and cast into an underground dungeon known as the Siyáh-Chál (Black Pit). Here He spent four months, laden with notorious chains so heavy that they left permanent marks on His body. With His feet in stocks, He was now companion to robbers and murderers. He was given no food for three days and nights, and sleep was almost impossible in that damp, cold, vermin-infested hole. An attempt was made to poison Him. Although it failed, His health remained impaired for years to come.

According to Bahá'í sources, it was in the gloom of the Black Pit, and under such appalling circumstances, that the Holy Spirit, symbolized in Zoroastrianism by the Sacred Fire, in Judaism by the Burning Bush, in Christianity by the Dove, and in Islam by the Archangel Gabriel, descended upon Bahá'u'lláh in the form of a celestial female being whom He identified as the "Maiden" or the "Maid of Heaven." Through Her, He learned that He was the new messenger of God for our age and began to receive His first revelations from God.

Although Bahá'u'lláh's innocence in the assassination attempt was eventually established, He was banished from Persia for promoting the Faith of the Báb. All His belongings were confiscated; His house and possessions were pillaged. This banishment from His native land ushered in a period of forty years of exile, imprisonment, and persecution for Bahá'u'lláh. First, He and His family were sent to Baghdad in neighboring Iraq, then under the jurisdiction of the Ottoman Empire.

Having lived in Baghdad for about a year, Bahá'u'lláh left for the mountainous wilderness of Kurdistan, where He lived a solitary life for two years. He spent this period of solitude reflecting on the implications of the mighty task to which He had been called. This period in His life is reminiscent of the periods of seclusion undertaken by some of the Founders of the other great religions in preparation for their prophetic missions. It recalls the wanderings of Buddha, Zoroaster's seclusion on Mount Ushidam, the forty days and nights spent by Jesus in the wilderness, and Muhammad's retreat in the caves of Mount Hirá.

Bahá'u'lláh returned to Baghdad in 1856. There, under His renewed leadership, the stature of the Bábí community-in-exile grew. Bahá'u'lláh's reputation as a spiritual teacher spread throughout Baghdad and the neighboring areas; princes, government officials, mystics, and scholars came to meet Him and hear His teachings. While in Baghdad He revealed a number of books including His two most well-known mystical works, the Hidden Words, and the Seven Valleys. But His growing fame created fear and suspicion in the minds of the King of Persia and his government, who pressed the Ottoman authorities to banish Him further from the borders of Iran, to the city of Istanbul, the capital of the Empire.

In April 1863, on the eve of their departure from Baghdad, Bahá'u'lláh and His companions camped in a garden on an island on the banks of the Tigris River, now known to Bahá'ís as the Garden of Riḍván (Paradise). Here He spent twelve days, bidding farewell to the community and other friends. It was in that garden that Bahá'u'lláh announced to the inner circle of His companions that He was indeed the Universal Messenger of God foretold by the Báb and by all the religions of the past. For Bahá'ís, this proclamation laid the foundation stone of a new world civilization. It is the "Great Announcement" expected and longed for by the followers of all the world religions. This is why it is this event (and not the birthday of Bahá'u'lláh) that is celebrated in the Bahá'í calendar as the "Most Great Festival," the most significant commemorative occasion of the year.

Bahá'u'lláh stayed in Istanbul for only four months before being forced into further exile, this time to Adrianople (modern Edirne) in Turkey. He lived here for five years, before being sent to His final place of exile – 'Akká (Acre, St. Jean d'Acre), then a penal city in Ottoman Palestine, now part of Israel. 'Akká was chosen mainly because Bahá'u'lláh's enemies believed He could not survive the experience. In the 1860s it was a pestilential place, a final destination for murderers, thieves, highway robbers and political dissidents from all parts of the Ottoman Empire. The city had no source of fresh water; it was damp, filthy, infested with fleas, and rife with disease.

It was into such an environment that Bahá'u'lláh and His family arrived in the August of 1868. Initially confined to prison in the barracks, Bahá'u'lláh and His companions were moved after two years to a cramped house in the city in order to make room for more troops.

During the last year of His stay in Adrianople and the first years in 'Akká, Bahá'u'lláh sent a number of letters (Tablets) to the secular and religious rulers of the time, including Pope Pius IX, Napoleon III of France, Alexander II of Russia, William I of Germany, Franz Josef of Austria, Queen Victoria of England, Sultan 'Abdu'l-'Azíz of Turkey, and Násíri-Dín Sháh of Persia. In these letters, Bahá'u'lláh publicly proclaimed Himself to be the Savior expected by the adherents of many different religions. Also, He called on world leaders to reduce their armaments, to concern themselves with the plight of the poor and oppressed in their countries and to rule with justice and equity. He also invited the rulers to unite in the creation of a body of international governance composed of representatives of all the nations, and to act unitedly to overcome war and tyranny, in a system of collective security. None of the letters received any substantial response from their addressees; over time, however, the counsels in them have begun to attract attention.

In 'Akká, Bahá'u'lláh and His companions were at first viewed as dangerous heretics and so encountered much animosity from the inhabitants. This gradually changed, as Bahá'u'lláh's innocence of any crime was soon recognized by most. Several officials antagonistic toward the exiles were also gradually replaced by more friendly administrators, including the Governor of 'Akká. Additionally, in their dealings with the

Bahá'ís, particularly with 'Abdu'l-Bahá, the residents of the city were impressed with the kindness and integrity displayed by the followers of the "Persian Prophet."

The restrictions on Bahá'u'lláh and His companions were thus relaxed over time and the flow of pilgrims swelled. Many notables, including several area governors and clerics, became admirers. Over the next twenty years, while officially still a prisoner of the Ottoman Emperor, Bahá'u'lláh continued to reveal the teachings and laws of the new religion. These were gradually distributed to His followers in both Persia and the different parts of the Ottoman Empire.

In the early part of May 1892, having contracted a slight fever, Bahá'u'lláh grew progressively weaker and eventually passed away in the early morning hours of 29 May at the age of 75. His remains were laid to rest in a garden room near 'Akká. This Shrine is now considered by Bahá'ís as the holiest place on the planet.

The teachings of Bahá'u'lláh have continued to spread around the world, and the Bahá'í Faith is now the most wide-spread religion after Christianity, although still numerically small. Most of Bahá'u'lláh's teachings on social questions – such as universal education, human rights, gender equality, removal of discrimination based on race, colour, sex or religion, respect for the environment, efforts to overcome extreme poverty and to recognize the spiritual value of work in contributing to human dignity, and so on – have become established in the 20th and 21st centuries as standards for civilized nations and peoples. Increasing acceptance of His moral, ethical and spiritual teachings is providing the foundation for success in implementing the social teachings. After all, the spiritual and ethical teachings are basically not new; they are, Bahá'is believe, the "ancient path cleared of superstitions" – the same eternal truths taught by all past religions, renewed in the present age by a new revelation from God.

Bibliography

Bahá'í Prayers, A Selection of Prayers Revealed by Bahá'u'lláh, the Báb, and 'Abdu'l-Bahá. Wilmette, IL: Bahá'í Publishing Trust, 2002.

The Bahá'ís: A Profile of the Bahá'í Faith and Its Worldwide Community. London: Bahá'í Publishing Trust, 1992. Website: www. bahai.org

Bahá'u'lláh. *Epistle to the Son of the Wolf.* Trans. Shoghi Effendi. Wilmette, IL: Bahá'í Publishing Trust, 1988.

— *Gleanings from the Writings of Bahá'u'lláh.* Trans. Shoghi Effendi. Wilmette, IL: Bahá'í Publishing Trust, 1994.

— *The Hidden Words of Bahá'u'lláh.* Trans. Shoghi Effendi. Wilmette, IL: Bahá'í Publishing Trust, 1990.

— *The Kitáb-i-Aqdas: The Most Holy Book.* Haifa: Bahá'í World Centre, 1992.

— *The Kitáb-i-Iqán: The Book of Certitude.* Trans. Shoghi Effendi. Wilmette, IL: Bahá'í Publishing Trust, 1993.

— *Prayers and Meditations by Bahá'u'lláh.* Trans. Shoghi Effendi. Wilmette, IL: Bahá'í Publishing Trust, 1987.

— *The Summons of the Lord of Hosts: Tablets of Bahá'u'lláh.* Haifa: Bahá'í World Centre, 2002.

— *Tablets of Bahá'u'lláh Revealed after the Kitáb-i-Aqdas.* Trans. Habib Taherzadeh. Haifa: Bahá'í World Centre, 1978; Wilmette, IL: Bahá'í Publishing Trust, 1988.

Bainton, R. H. *Christianity.* Boston: Houghton Mifflin, 1964.

Beaver, R. P., et al. (eds.). *Eerdmans' Handbook to the World's Religions.* Grand Rapids: William B. Eerdmans, 1982.

The Bhagavad Gita. Trans. J. Mascaro. New York: Penguin, 1962.

Bhaktivedanta Swami Prabhupáda, A. C. *KRSNA: The Supreme Personality of Godhead.* New York: The Bhaktivedanta Book Trust, 1970.

The Bible. *The Holy Bible: Revised Standard Version*. New York: Thomas Nelson & Sons, 1952.

Bowker, J. (ed.). *The Oxford Dictionary of World Religions*. Oxford: Oxford University Press, 1997.

Boyce, M. *Zoroastrians: Their Religious Beliefs and Practices*. New York: Routledge & Kegan Paul, 1985.

Buddhist Suttas. Trans. T.W. Rhys Davids. F. M. Müller (ed.), *Sacred Books of the East*, Vol. XI (1881).

Buddhist Texts: Through the Ages. Trans. and ed. E. Conze. Oxford: Bruno Cassirer, 1954. Boston: Shambhala, 1990.

al-Bukharí, Muhammad ibn Isma'il (810–87). *Mukhtasar sahih al-Bukharí: jam' al-nihayah fi bad' al-khayr wa-ghayah*. Cairo, 1982.

Carus, P. *The Gospel of Buddha*. Chicago and London: Open Court, 1894.

Coward, H. *Pluralism in the World Religions: A Short Introduction*. Oxford: OneWorld, 2000.

Crim, K.; Bullard, R. A.; Shinn, L. D. (eds.). *Abingdon Dictionary of Living Religions*. Nashville: Parthenon Press, 1981.

The Dhammapada: The Path to Perfection. Trans. J. Mascaro. New York: Penguin, 1973.

Digha Nikaya. *The Long Discourses of the Buddha: A Translation of the Digha Nikaya*. Trans. M. Walsh. Boston: Wisdom Publications, 1995.

Eck, D. *A New Religious America: How a "Christian Country" Has Become the World's Most Religiously Diverse Nation*. San Francisco: Harper & Row, 2002.

— *Encountering God: A Spiritual Journey from Bozeman to Banaras*. Boston: Beacon Press, 1994.

Eliade, M. *A History of Religious Ideas*. 3 vols. *I: From the Stone Age to the Eleusinian Mysteries. II: From Gautama Buddha to the Triumph of*

Christianity. III: From Muhammad to the Age of Reforms. Chicago: University of Chicago Press, 1978–85.

— ; Couliano, I. *The Eliade Guide to World Religions.* New York: Harper Collins, 1991.

Esposito, J. L. *Islam: The Straight Path.* Oxford: Oxford University Press, 1998.

Fieser, J; Powers, J. *Scriptures of the West.* Boston: McGraw Hill, 1998.

Fisher, M. P. *Living Religions: A Brief Introduction.* Upper Saddle River, NJ: Prentice Hall, 2002.

— ; Luyster, R. *Living Religions: An Encyclopedia of the World's Faiths.* London, New York: I. B. Tauris, 1990.

Fo-Sho-Hing-Tsan-King. Life of Buddha by Asvaghosha Bodhisdattva. Trans. S. Beal. F. M. Müller (ed.), *Sacred Books of the East*, Vol. XIX (1883).

Glasse, C. *The Concise Encyclopedia of Islam.* San Francisco: Harper & Row, 1989.

Guillaume, A. *The Life of Muhammad: A Translation of Ishaq's Sirat Rasul Allah.* Oxford, London: Oxford University Press, 1982.

Hatcher, W. S.; Martin, D. J. *The Bahá'í Faith: The Emerging Global Religion.* San Francisco: Harper & Row, 1984.

Herrmann, Siegfried. *Israel In Egypt.* Naperville, Ill.: Alec R. Allenson, 1973.

Hick, J. *An Interpretation of Religion: Human Responses to the Transcendent.* New Haven: Yale University Press, 1989.

— *God and the Universe of Faiths.* Glasgow: Collins, 1977.

— *God Has Many Names.* Philadelphia: The Westminster Press, 1982.

— *The Metaphor of God Incarnate: Christology in a Pluralistic Age.* Louisville: Westminster/John Knox Press. 1993.

— (ed.). *The Myth of God Incarnate.* London: SCM Press, 1977.

— (ed.). *Problems of Religious Pluralism.* New York: St. Martin's Press, 1985.

Hopfe, L. M.; Woodward, M. R. *Religions of the World*. Upper Saddle River, NJ: Prentice Hall, 1998.

Humphreys, C. *Buddhism: An Introduction and Guide*. New York: Penguin, 1988.

The Hymns of Zarathustra. Trans. M. Henning. Rutland, Vt.: Charles E. Tuttle, 1992.

Jackson, A. V. Williams. *Zoroaster: The Prophet of Ancient Iran*. New York: AMS Press, 1965.

Knitter, P. *Jesus and the Other Names: Christian Mission and Global Responsibility*. Maryknoll, NY: Orbis Books, 2001.
— *No Other Name?* Maryknoll, NY: Orbis Books, 1985.

Küng, H. *Global Responsibility: In Search of a New World Ethic*. New York: Continuum, 1991.
— et al. *Christianity and the World Religions: Paths to Dialogue with Islam, Hinduism, and Buddhism*. Garden City, NY: Doubleday, 1986.

Luce, H. (ed.). *The World's Great Religions*. New York: Time Inc., 1957.

Majjhima Nikaya. *The Middle Length Discourses of the Buddha: A New Translation of the Majjhima Nikaya*. Trans. Bhikku Nanamoli. Boston: Wisdom Publications, 1995.

Marks, G. W. *Call to Remembrance: Connecting the Heart to Bahá'u'lláh*. Wilmette, IL: Bahá'í Publishing Trust, 1992.

Masefield, P. *Divine Revelation in Pali Buddhism*. Colombo: Sri Lanka Institute of Traditional Studies, 1986.

Maʿṣúmián, F. *Life After Death: A Study of the Afterlife in World Religions*. Los Angeles: Kalimát Press, 2002.

Momen, M. "Bahá'u'lláh's prophetology: Archetypal patterns in the lives of the founders of the world religions," in *Bahá'í Studies Review* (London), 1995, vol. 5, No. 1, pp. 51–63.
— *Hinduism and the Bahá'í Faith*. Oxford: George Ronald, 1990.

Mǘller, F. M. (ed.). *Sacred Books of the East*. Various translators. Vols. I–L. Oxford: Clarendon Press, 1879–1910.

Nabíl-i-A'ẓam (Muhammad-i-Zarandi). *The Dawn-Breakers: Nabíl's Narrative of the Early Days of the Bahá'í Revelation*. Trans. Shoghi Effendi. Wilmette, IL: Bahá'í Publishing Trust, 1970.

Nigosian, S. A. *World Faiths*. New York: St. Martin's Press, 1994.

Noss, D. S.; Noss, J. B. *A History of the World's Religions*. New York: Macmillan College Publishing Company, 1994.

Oxtoby, W. G. *World Religions: Eastern Traditions*. Toronto: Oxford University Press, 1996.

Panikkar, R. "Religious Pluralism: The Metaphysical Challenge", in Leroy S. Rouner (ed.), *Religious Pluralism*. Boston University Studies in Philosophy and Religion, vol. 5. Notre Dame: University of Notre Dame Press, 1984, pp. 97–115.
— *The Unknown Christ of Hinduism*. Maryknoll, NY: Orbis Books, 1981.

Qur'án. *The Koran*. Trans. J. M. Rodwell. New York: Ivy Books, 1993.

Samyutta Nikaya. *The Book of the Kindred Sayings*. 5 vols. Trans. C. A. F. Rhys Davids and F. L. Woodward. London: Pali Text Society, 1917–30.

Saunders, K. J. *Gotama Buddha: A Biography Based on Canonical Books of the Theravadin*. New York: Association Press, 1920.

Schaefer, U. *Beyond the Clash of Religions: The Emergence of a New Paradigm*. Prague: Zero Palm Press, 1998.

Seager, R. H. (ed.). *The Dawn of Religious Pluralism: Voices from the World's Parliament of Religions, 1893*. La Salle, Ill.: Open Court, 1993.

Sen, K. M. *Hinduism*. London: Penguin, 1987.

Shoghi Effendi. *God Passes By* (1941). Wilmette, IL: Bahá'í Publishing Trust, rev. edn. 1995.

Smith, W. Cantwell. *Towards a World Theology: Faith and the Comparative History of Religion*. Louisville, KY: Westminster Press, 1981.

Songs of Zarathustra: The Gathas. Trans. Dastur Framroze Ardeshir Bode and Piloo Nanavutty. London: George Allen & Unwin, 1952.

Sours, M. W. *A Study of Bahá'u'lláh's Tablet to the Christians*. Oxford: Oneworld, 1990.

Universal House of Justice, The. *One Common Faith*. Haifa: Bahá'í World Centre, 2005.

Vinaya Texts. Part I: The Patimokkha, The Mahavagga, I-IV. Trans. T. W. Rhys Davis and H. Oldenberg. F. M. Müller (ed.), *Sacred Books of the East*, Vol. XIII (1881). New Delhi: Motilal Banarsidass, 1965.

Vincent, K. R. *The Magi: From Zoroaster to the Three Wise Men*. North Richland Hills, TX: Bibal Press, 1999.

Wilson, A. (ed.). *World Scripture: A Comparative Anthology of Sacred Texts*. New York: Paragon House, 1995.

Yasna. See *The Hymns of Zarathustra* and *Songs of Zarathustra*.

Zafrulla Khan, Muhammad. *Muhammad: Seal of the Prophets*. London: Routledge & Kegan Paul, 1980.

Zend-Avesta. Part 1. Trans. J. Darmesteter. F. M. Müller (ed.), *Sacred Books of the East*, Vol. IV (1880).

References and Notes

Preface

1. Seager, *The Dawn of Religious Pluralism*, p. 15.
2. ibid. pp. 15–16.
3. W. Cantwell Smith. *Towards a World Theology: Faith and the Comparative History of Religion.* Louisville, KY: Westminster Press, 1981.
4. The Universal House of Justice, *One Common Faith*, p. 16.
5. A. Wilson (ed.). *World Scripture: A Comparative Anthology of Sacred Texts.* New York, NY: Paragon House, 1995.

Advents: Their Appearance Prophesied

1. Yasna 46.1, in *Hymns of Zarathustra.*
2. Zend Avesta, p. 208.
3. Exod. 3: 11.
4. ibid. 4: 12–13.
5. Digha Nikaya i.115, in *Long Discourses*, p. 127.
6. Carus, *Gospel of Buddha*, pp. 36, 39. Adapted from Fo-Sho-Hing-Tran-King, vv. 1026–1100.
7. Luke 4: 1–13.
8. al-Bukharí 1: 3.
9. Qur'án 22: 52–3.
10. ibid. 10: 94.
11. Nabíl-i-A'ẓam, *Dawn-Breakers*, p. 585.
12. Bahá'u'lláh, Kitáb-i-Íqán, para. 278 (pp. 250–51).

Prophetic Call

1. Carus, *Gospel of Buddha*, p. 36. Adapted from Fo-Sho-Hing-Tsan-King, vv. 1026–9.
2. Yasna 43: 7–9, 15, in *Songs of Zarathustra.*
3. Exod. 3: 1–12.
4. Matt. 3: 13–17.
5. Qur'án 97: 1–5.

6. ibid. 96: 1–5.
7. Bahá'u'lláh, Súriy-i-Haykal (Surih of the Temple), paras. 6–7, in *Summons*, pp. 5–6.
8. Bahá'u'lláh, Lawḥ-i-Sulṭán, in Súriy-i-Haykal, para. 192, in *Summons*, p. 98.
9. Bahá'u'lláh, *Gleanings* XLI.

Their Dual Nature

1. Bahá'u'lláh, Kitáb-i-Íqán, paras. 191–4, passim (pp. 176–8).
2. Bhagavad Gita 7: 5.
3. ibid. 7: 24.
4. ibid. 7: 25–6.
5. ibid. 9: 13.
6. ibid. 10: 3.
7. ibid. 10: 33.
8. ibid. 10: 40.
9. Samyutta Nikaya iii: 120, in *Kindred Sayings.*
10. *Buddhist Suttas*, vol. II, p. 186.
11. Samyutta Nikaya, in *Buddhist Texts*, vol. 3, p. 118.
12. Anguttara Nikaya, ii: 37–9, in *Buddhist Texts.*
13. Deut. 29: 2, 5–6.
14. Exod. 4: 16.
15. Exod. 7: 1.
16. Num. 12: 6–8.
17. John 8: 58.
18. Rev. 21: 6.
19. John 17: 5.
20. ibid. 10: 30.
21. ibid. 10: 38
22. ibid. 14: 7–10.
23. ibid. 16: 15.
24. Mark 9: 37.
25. John 1: 1–3.
26. Qur'án 48: 10.
27. ibid. 4: 82.
28. Hadith, from the collections of Bukhari and Muslim, in Wilson, *World Scripture*, p. 465.
29. ibid. p. 466.
30. Bahá'u'lláh, Kitáb-i-Íqán, para. 196 (p. 178).
31. Bahá'u'lláh, Kitáb-i-Aqdas, para. 86.
32. ibid. para. 132.

33. Bahá'u'lláh, *Gleanings*, XXX.
34. ibid. XXI.
35. Bhagavad Gita 9: 11.
36. ibid. 11: 41–2.
37. Num. 12: 3.
38. Matt. 11: 27.
39. Mark 10: 18.
40. John 5: 29.
41. ibid. 7: 16.
42. ibid. 8: 28–9.
43. ibid. 8: 42.
44. ibid. 12: 49–50.
45. ibid. 14: 28.
46. ibid. 14: 31.
47. ibid. 5: 18.
48. Acts 2: 22.
49. Matt. 13: 53–5.
50. Qur'án 18: 110.
51. ibid. 3: 138.
52. Bahá'u'lláh, Suríy-i-Mulúk, para. 101, in *Summons*, p. 228, and *Gleanings* CXXIII: 17.
53. Bahá'u'lláh, *Gleanings* XLIX.

Their Unity

1. Bahá'u'lláh, *Gleanings* XIX: 3.
2. Milandapanha, p. 285, in *Buddhist Texts*, vol. 3, p. 118.
3. Rev. 21: 6.
4. John 5: 45–6.
5. Matt. 17: 12–13.
6. John 15: 26–7.
7. Qurán 2: 130.
8. ibid. 4: 151.
9. ibid. 41: 43.
10. ibid. 4: 149–50.
11. Bahá'u'lláh, *Gleanings* XXXIV: 3.
12. ibid. XIX: 4.
13. ibid. XXIV.
14. Bahá'u'lláh, Kitáb-i-Íqán, para. 162, pp. 153–4.

Revealers of Truth

1. Momen, "Bahá'u'lláh's prophetology," p. 56.

2. Bhagavad Gita 3: 3.
3. ibid. 8: 13.
4. ibid. 3: 31–2.
5. ibid. 9: 17–18.
6. ibid. 10: 32.
7. From rGya Tchee Roll Pa, *Histoire du Buddha Sakya Mouni* (Foucaux, Paris 1868), in Carus, p. 163.
8. Dhammapada, v. 190.
9. Digha Nikaya i: 249, 252.
10. Dhammapada, vv. 273–5.
11. ibid. v. 45.
12. ibid. v. 115.
13. Yasna 50: 6.
14. ibid. 46: 3.
15. ibid. 53: 1.
16. ibid. 53: 2.
17. ibid. 43: 3.
18. ibid. 48: 3.
19. ibid. 45: 5.
20. Exod. 24: 12–13, 15, 17–18.
21. Lev. 19: 1–2.
22. Exod. 29: 45–6.
23. John 1: 18.
24. I John 2: 22–3.
25. Mark 2: 27–8.
26. Matt. 5: 31–2.
27. ibid. 5: 38–40.
28. ibid. 5: 43–6.
29. ibid. 5: 48.
30. ibid. 5: 3–12.
31. John 14: 6.
32. Acts 4: 12.
33. John 10: 9.
34. Qur'án 33: 43–4.
35. ibid. 24: 53.
36. ibid. 42: 51–3.
37. ibid. 17: 84.
38. ibid. 2: 23.
39. ibid. 3: 79.
40. ibid. 3: 17.
41. ibid. 5: 3.

42. Bahá'u'lláh, Tablet of Aḥmad, in *Bahá'í Prayers*, p. 210.
43. Bahá'u'lláh, *Gleanings* XLIII: 3.
44. ibid. LXX: 3.
45. ibid. CXXIX: 5.
46. Bahá'u'lláh, Lawḥ-i-Maqṣúd, in *Tablets*, p. 169.
47. Bahá'u'lláh, Kitáb-i-Aqdas, para. 1.
48. Bahá'u'lláh, Tablet of Aḥmad, in *Bahá'í Prayers*, p. 212.
49. Bahá'u'lláh, *Gleanings* CV: 1.

The Light that Shineth in Darkness

1. Bhagavad Gita 13: 17.
2. ibid 8: 9–10.
3. ibid. 10: 12.
4. ibid. 11: 12.
5. ibid. 13: 33.
6. ibid. 11: 47.
7. ibid. 15: 12.
8. Samyutta Nikaya: 442, in *Kindred Sayings*, vol. 5, p. 374.
9. Psalms 27: 1.
10. ibid. 119: 105.
11. Prov. 6: 23.
12. Isa. 60: 19–20.
13. Jas. 1: 17.
14. I John 1: 15.
15. John 1: 6–10.
16. ibid. 3–19.
17. 2 Cor. 4–6.
18. Rev. 21: 23.
19. John 9: 5.
20. ibid. 12: 46.
21. ibid. 8: 12.
22. ibid. 12: 35–6.
23. Qur'án 24 (Surah al-Núr).
24. ibid. 24: 35.
25. ibid. 4: 174.
26. ibid. 61: 8
27. ibid. 7: 157.
28. ibid. 64: 8.
29. ibid. 42: 52.
30. ibid. 5: 15–18.
31. ibid. 14: 1.

32. ibid. 5: 48.
33. ibid. 6: 91.
34. ibid. 21: 49.
35. Bahá'u'lláh, in *Prayers and Meditations*, pp. 269–70.
36. ibid. p. 193.
37. Bahá'u'lláh, Hidden Words, Arabic 12.
38. Bahá'u'lláh, in *Prayers and Meditations*, p. 336.
39. Bahá'u'lláh, *Gleanings* XC: 1.
40. Bahá'u'lláh, Ṭarázát, para. 2, in *Tablets*, p. 33.
41. Bahá'u'lláh, I<u>sh</u>ráqát, para. 34, in *Tablets*, p. 119.
42. Bahá'u'lláh, Lawḥ-i-Aqdas (Tablet to the Christians), para. 17, in *Tablets*, p. 14.
43. Baha'u'lláh, *Prayers and Meditations*, p. 153.
44. Bahá'u'lláh, Lawḥ-i-Aqdas, para. 13, in *Tablets*, p. 13.
45. Bahá'u'lláh, *Gleanings* CLXII: 2.
46. Bahá'u'lláh, *Prayers and Meditations*, p. 218.
47. Bahá'u'lláh, Súriy-i-Haykal, para. 133, in *Summons*, p. 68.
48. Bahá'u'lláh, I<u>sh</u>ráqát, para. 3, in *Tablets*, p. 102.
49. ibid. para. 14, in *Tablets*, p. 108.
50. Bahá'u'lláh, Kitáb-i-Aqdas, para. 85.

Rejection by Humanity

1. Bhagavad Gita 7: 3.
2. Dhammapada 320.
3. Yasna 46: 1–3, in *The Hymns of Zarathustra.*
4. Exod. 14: 10–12.
5. ibid. 16: 2–3.
6. Num. 14: 1–3.
7. ibid. 16: 13.
8. Matt. 8: 19–20.
9. ibid. 11: 18–19.
10. ibid. 13: 53–7.
11. John 10: 20.
12. Mark 14: 61–2, 64–5.
13. John 18: 22–3.
14. Matt. 26: 67.
15. Mark 15: 16–20.
16. Qur'án 5: 74.
17. ibid. 37: 35.
18. ibid. 36: 30.
19. ibid. 40: 5.

20. ibid. 2: 85.
21. ibid. 34: 43.
22. ibid. 25: 30.
23. ibid. 68: 1–7.
24. ibid. 17: 45–6.
25. Bahá'u'lláh, Epistle to the Son of the Wolf, pp. 76–7.
26. Bahá'u'lláh, Kitáb-i-Íqán, para. 208 (p. 190).
27. Bahá'u'lláh, *Prayers and Meditations*, p. 302.
28. Bahá'u'lláh, Súriy-i-Muluk, para. 100, in *Summons*, p. 227; and *Gleanings* CXVIII.
29. ibid. para. 81, in *Summons*, pp. 218–19; and *Gleanings* CXIV.
30. Bahá'u'lláh, Epistle to the Son of the Wolf, p. 52.

Opposition of the Divines

1. Yasna 32: 15, in *The Hymns of Zarathustra.*
2. ibid. 51: 14.
3. Majjhima Nikaya i: 140, in *Middle Length Discourses*, p. 234, no. 37.
4. Samyutta Nikaya iv: 117f, in Masefield, *Divine Revelation in Pali Buddhism*, p. 154.
5. Matt. 5: 20.
6. ibid. 21: 30–31.
7. ibid. 23: 1–7.
8. ibid. 23: 13, 15.
9. ibid. 23: 26–7.
10. ibid. 23: 28, 33.
11. Luke 11: 42–4.
12. Matt. 27: 20–24.
13. Qur'án 9: 34–5.
14. ibid. 33: 67–8
15. ibid. 5: 67.
16. Bahá'u'lláh, Kitáb-i-Aqdas, para. 167.
17. Bahá'u'lláh, in *Gleanings* XXIII: 1–3.
18. Bahá'u'lláh, Kitáb-i-Íqán, paras. 236–7 (pp. 213–14).
19. ibid. para. 15 (p. 15).

Sacrificial Lambs

1. Dhammapada 320.
2. Yasna 43: 11, in *The Hymns of Zarathustra.*
3. Deut. 9: 15–18, 25–6.
4. ibid. 3: 26–7.

5. ibid. 4: 21–2.
6. Luke 23: 33.
7. Matt. 26: 28.
8. Rom. 5: 8.
9. John 1: 29.
10. John 10: 11–13.
11. Qur'án 6: 33.5.
12. Bahá'u'lláh, Kitáb-i-Íqán, paras. 115–16 (pp. 109–10).
13. Bahá'u'lláh, *Gleanings* C: 6.
14. ibid. CXLI: 2.
15. Bahá'u'lláh, Lawḥ-i-Aqdas (Tablet to the Christians), para. 8, in *Tablets*, p. 12.
16. Bahá'u'lláh, *Gleanings* XLV.
17. Bahá'u'lláh, Lawḥ-i-Aqdas (Tablet to the Christians), para. 5, in *Tablets*, p. 10.
18. Bahá'u'lláh, *Gleanings* XLV.

Continuity with the Past

1. Bhagavad Gita 4: 1–3.
2. Samyutta Nikaya ii: 104, in *Kindred Sayings*, vol. 2, p. 74.
3. Exod. 3: 15.
4. John 5: 45–6.
5. Matt. 5: 17–18.
6. Heb. 1: 1–2.
7. Qur'án 41: 43.
8. ibid. 4: 163.
9. ibid. 3: 180.
10. ibid. 42: 11.
11. Bahá'u'lláh, Kitáb-i-Aqdas, para. 182.
12. Bahá'u'lláh, *Gleanings* XXX.
13. ibid. XXII.
14. ibid. XXXIV: 3.

Future Saviors

1. Bhagavad Gita 4: 7–8.
2. Farvardin Yasht 13: 129, in Wilson, *World Scripture*, p. 785.
3. Digha Nikaya ii: 76, in *Long Discourses*, pp. 403–4.
4. Mahaparinibbana Suttanta (The Book of the Great Decease), in *Buddhist Suttas*; quoted in Carus, *Gospel of Buddha*, p. 245.
5. Deut. 18: 15.
6. ibid. 18: 17–19.

7. Dan. 7: 13–14.
8. Isa. 9: 6–7.
9. ibid. 2: 4.
10. ibid. 11: 6.
11. ibid. 66: 18.
12. John 16: 12–15.
13. Jesus preferred the title "Son of man" not "Son of God" for Himself. The New Testament contains only a few references to Jesus as the Son of God. The most significant examples are perhaps Matt. 26: 63–8 and John 5: 25. In Matthew, shortly before the crucifixion and in response to pressure from the High Priest who asks Jesus point-blank if He is Christ, the Son of God, Jesus confirms that He is ("Thou hast said") but, even there, He immediately follows this by calling Himself by His preferred title (Son of man). On the contrary, there are well over 100 places in the New Testament where Jesus calls Himself the Son of man. For a few examples, see Matt. 11:19, 12: 8, 12: 32, 16: 13, 16: 27; Mark 2: 10, 2: 28, 8: 31, 8: 38, 9: 9; Luke 5: 24, 6: 22, 7: 34, 9: 22, 9: 26; and John 1: 51, 3: 13, 3: 14, 5: 27. By accepting the "Son of man" as a designation, Jesus was in fact continuing the Hebrew tradition of prophets and holy figures assuming that title. Jews were already familiar with this appellation. In Chapters 8 and 11 through 47 of Ezekiel, God calls Ezekiel "Son of man" 118 times! Daniel also used the same designation for the future prophet whose advent he foresaw in a vision (7: 13).
14. Matt. 24: 37–44.
15. ibid. 25: 13.
16. Mark 13: 32.
17. Matt. 24: 21, 29–31.
18. Rev. 21: 1–2, 10–11, 23–26.
19. Qur'án 7: 35.
20. ibid. 2: 38–9.
21. Numerous other passages in the Qur'án refer to Islam and other religions as different "nations," "peoples," or "communities" (Arabic word "Umma"). For example, see Qur'án 2: 143, 3: 104, 7: 181, 13: 30, 16: 120, 22: 67.
22. Qur'án 10: 47.
23. ibid. 35: 24
24. ibid. 7: 34.
25. ibid. 23: 43.
26. ibid. 2: 138.
27. Bahá'u'lláh, *Gleanings* XXVII: 6.

28. Bahá'u'lláh, Kitáb-i-Aqdas, para. 37.
29. Bahá'u'lláh,, *Gleanings* III: 1.
30. ibid. III: 2.
31. ibid. VI: 1.
32. ibid. VII: 1.
33. ibid. VII: 2.
34. Bahá'u'lláh,, Kitáb-i-Aqdas, para. 80.
35. Bahá'u'lláh, *Gleanings* XVII: 2.

Brief Lives of the Divine Educators

1. Rig Veda 21, 164, 46.
2. Bhagavad Gita 4: 7–8.
3. Bhaktivedanta Swami Prabhupáda, *KRSNA*, pp. 1–11.
4. Fisher, *Living Religions*, p. 68.
5. Ma'ṣúmián, *Life After Death*, p. 11.
6. Bhagavad Gita 9: 30–32.
7. ibid. 2: 18, 24.
8. ibid. 9: 17–34.
9. Gen. 15: 7.
10. Matt. 26: 64.
11. Among the Jews, belief in the prophets' ability to perform supernatural acts, including resurrecting the dead and curing leprosy and blindness, pre-dates Jesus by many centuries. The Bible confirms that both Elijah and his successor Elishah (who lived some 900 years before Jesus) performed similar miracles. According to I Kings: 17, Elijah restored the life of a dead boy while Elishah raised the son of the Shunammite woman from the dead (II Kings 4: 18-37) and healed Naaman, the commander of the Syrian army, of leprosy (2 Kings 5: 1-19, Luke 4: 27). Elishah also restored sight to others (II Kings 6: 20) and, on a different occasion, afflicted the whole Syrian army with blindness (II Kings 6: 18). The Bible claims that even after Elishah's death his sacred bones continued to have the power to restore life to the dead (II King 6: 18).
12. I Cor. 15: 42–45.
13. Qur'án 96: 1–5.
14. The Black Stone (*al-hajarul aswad* in Arabic) is a holy relic in Islam and has been a fixture in the Ka'bah for centuries. It is oval in shape and the size of a pomegranate. It is the cornerstone of the southeast corner of the Ka'bah. While circumambulating (*tawaf*) the Ka'bah and as a part of the pilgrimage ritual (*hajj*), Muslims try to stop and kiss the Black Stone. Muslim and non-Muslim sources alike

agree that the Stone was an object of veneration in pre-Islamic days, but opinions vary on its origins and significance. Secular historians believe the veneration of the Black Stone to be rooted in the pre-Islamic practice of meteorite worship. Many ancient cultures, including pagan Arabs, engaged in meteorite worship because they were convinced these stones had magical powers by virtue of descending from the skies, the habitation of gods.

Muslims hold divergent, even conflicting, views on the history and significance of the Black Stone. Some claim the Stone was found by the great patriarch Abraham and His son Ishmael when they were looking for stones to build the original Ka'bah, centuries before Muhammad's time. Other Muslims go so far as to attribute supernatural powers to the Black Stone, such as the power to absolve sins. They believe the Black Stone fell from the sky during the time of Adam, the first human and the first Prophet. Originally, it was pure and dazzling white, but because it had the power to absorb the sins of Muslim pilgrims, over centuries it gradually grew dark.

Other Muslims, observing the veneration of the Black Stone by their fellow believers, find the practice to be if not sheer idolatry (*shirk*), at least inconsistent with the Qur'anic injunction to worship only Allah. They also hold that granting a piece of stone the power to absolve humans of sins is not only inconsistent with Islamic teachings but defeats the Muslim argument against mainstream Christianity which grants such powers to Jesus (rather than God).

Still others, including Islam's second Caliph ('Umar) ascribed no sacred history or magical powers to the Black Stone. 'Umar did venerate and kiss the stone but only as a sign of trust in what he had seen Muhammad do before him:

> No doubt, I know that you are a stone and can neither harm anyone nor benefit anyone. Had I not seen Allah's Messenger kissing you, I would not have kissed you (al-Bukharí, vol. 1, book 26: 667, 675).

Muslim pilgrims often use the Black Stone to keep track of the number of circumambulations around the Ka'bah sanctuary.